BUMPER
BOOK OF
BOOBS

D1331646

This book contains the pick of
the misprints and other absurdities
culled from the press by **Private Eye.**
All the cuttings are genuine;
none has been altered.
The majority were sent in by readers,
to whom our thanks are due.
Included here are the best of those
published in two previous books,
but most of the material is new.

THERE were few bargains at the sale of Africans at Ashbey's Galleries yesterday morning. Bidding was fast and keen, and buyers showed little hesitancy in their bids.

Cape Times

BUMPER
BOOK OF
BOOBS

Illustrated by
Larry, Ralph Steadman and Bill Tidy

A Private Eye Book

Published in Great Britain in 1973 by
Private Eye Productions Limited,
6 Carlisle Street, London W1.

Published August 1973
Re-printed March 1974,
November 1974, September 1975,
April 1976, January 1977,
January 1979, October 1979,
January 1980, October 1980,
April 1981, August 1981,
November 1982, August 1983,
August 1984, April 1985,
October 1986, August 1987,
March 1988, January 1989,
September 1989 and January 1990

SBN 23396492 4

Made and printed in Great Britain by
Halstan & Co. Ltd., Amersham, Bucks., England

DEDICATION

To the typesetters of **The Grauniad**

Design: Stephen Pomfret

Cover Photography: Eric Stevens

HAROLD MACMILLAN

HORROR AT CORBY AND KETTERING

By JOHN PRINCE
Health Correspondent

Daily Telegraph

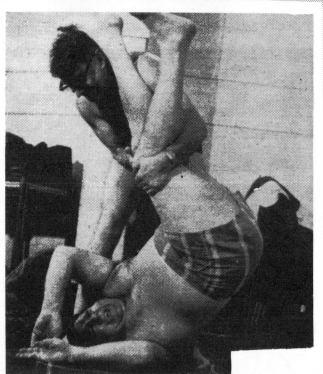

Selwyn Lloyd (left), Chancellor of the Exchequer in the Conservative Government 1960 to 1962, talks in *The Day Before Yesterday* about the first wage restraint policy.

TV Times

LINCOLNSHIRE
STANDARD

MARPLES ACCUSED OF 'COMPLETE EVASION'

HE SLEPT THROUGH AN EARTHQUAKE

DRAMA AT SKEGNESS CIRCUS

NET WEEKLY SALE 59,174

Nudist welfare model wife fell Chinese hypnot the Co-op bacc

News of the World

AMAZING RESULTS FRO WAIST REDUCER — M WOMEN ALIKE

Sunday Mirror

8

man's

for the

st from

factory

Jap with
parachute
skis down
Everest
on one leg
at 93 mph
and lives

Sun

NEW

AND

Massive
organ
draws
the crowd

Kent Messenger

9

von Kar, Nikobar, Reise der Novara
Seaton (Julia), Regeneration Through Farting
Semple (Allen), The Influence of Geographical
    Environment (1911)

The Clique

President Nixon sets off today on a tour of six Asian nations to explain his intentions and assure the countries that America is abandoning them to their enemies.

Daily Mail

I ASKED recently what Anne Boleyn had two more of than Gladstone. The answer was "Fingers." because she had six fingers on one hand, and Gladstone had one blown off in a shooting accident.

Now I am asked by Mr F. H. Bennett of West Wimbledon what else Anne Boleyn had two more of than Gladstone.

The answer is: **The letter N.** Well done Mr Bennett—and thank you very much.

Goldfish is saved from drowning

From Our Correspondent

Amersham, Aug. 12

An R.S.P.C.A. inspector tonight commended Mr. Peter Humphrey, aged 55, for saving a goldfish from drowning, and a full report of the rescue is to be sent to R.S.P.C.A. headquarters for consideration by the awards committee.

Times

The exhibition opens at 11 a.m. tomorrow, with the Chancellor of the Duchy of Lancaster, the Rt. Hon. Fred Hill, M.P. performing the opening ceremony in the crypt.

Evening Gazette

"From the point of view of the Highlands and Islands Development Board, 1968 was indeed an 'anus mirabilis,' rendered so particularly by the Government's decision to site British Aluminium's new smelter at Invergordon

Inverness Courier

west England and Berkeley reckons that a thousand or more Conservatives abstained from voting specifically because of the homosexual issue.

'I knew I was endangering my seat

Honeymoon? if we can fit it in, say couple

Northern Echo

Mounting problems for young couples

Speaking at a social evening

Western Gazette

Threatening letters –man asks for long sentence

Scotsman

Sultan falls to mildew epidemic

Suffolk Free Press

Dr James Pike, the former Anglican Bishop of California who died recently in Israel, talks to Oliver Hunkin about psychic phenomena

Miss Giavollela had pleaded guilty to stealing goods worth £25 0s. 2½d. from Tesco Supermarket; to assaulting a policewoman; and to dishonestly handling a garden gnome.

Oxford Mail

Frenzied Welcome Awaits
Britain's Lone Yachtsman

D.essed in an ash suit and wearing the familiar red-rose in his bottom-hole, Lt. General Afrifa appeared with Lt-General Ocran for the last time at the meeting room of the Council of State and declared that the Constitution was also an "insult" to the youth.

Pioneer (Ghana)

Mr Anthony Chenevix Trench, head of Eton, said the system provided for a great deal of participation by the boys. "I'm always available to boys of any age who want to see me. I've been put on the mat by quite young boys.'

Grauniad

On return journey home called at Silkstone W.M.C. where Con. Sec. Jack Hastey had his, and the Club's favourite, Beryl Burgess entertaining. Still as popular as ever with the audience. Organist Ivy was working under a great strain on this occasion having had a fall in the morning, but, being the kind of person she is, did not let the Club down even though she had to be lifted on and off the organ. Thanks Ivy.

The Voice of Clubland — Spotlight Magazine

15

Spanish dictator, Francisco Franco, took time off recently during a tour of the frequently rebellious province of Asturias to catch this large salmon.

The Standard of Tanzan

Sir Seewoosagur a dit "bolshy"

—

NOUS apprenons, dans les milieux de l'Assemblée législative, que l'audition de la bande magnétique a permis d'établir que c'est bien **bolshy** *et non* **bull-shit** *que Sir Seewoosagur a employé mardi, à la Chambre.*

Encore une fois, le Parti Mauricien aura trouvé une tempête dans un verre d'eau.

Advance (Mauritius)

These are some of the pictures on show at the Young Artists' Exhibition in Moscow's Central Exhibition Hall, one of the USSR's 50th anniversary events.

The 1,500 exhibits, displayed to the best advantage over nearly two acres, are the pick of 20,000 submitted by young painters, graphic artists and sculptors in every Soviet republic.

Nearly all were executed over the past two years or so.

MAKE-UP HINTS

Hints on making-up were given to members of the Leeds branch of the British Sailors' Society today by Mrs. W. Toulson, of Bedale. Mrs. Arthur Beevers presided.

Yorkshire Evening Post

YPAC RUGBY

1 FIJI

FIJIANS "LEARNED NOTHING" - EMBERSON

ALTHOUGH STANDARDS WERE HIGHER THAN EXPECTED, THE FIJIAN TEAM "LEARNED NOTHING" ON THEIR 14-MATCH TOUR OF ENGLAND AND WALES. THAT WAS THE VIEW OF DR. FELIX EMBERSON, THEIR ASSISTANT MANAGER AND JOINT COACH, BEFORE THE TEAM FLEW TO NEW YORK TODAY.

"WHEN WE GET HOME, THE FORWARDS WILL HAVE TO START ALL OVER AGAIN TO LEARN HOW TO FUCK. IT IS ABSURD THAT THE OUTLOOK ON THIS PART OF THE GAME IS COMPLETELY DIFFERENT IN THE NORTHERN AND SOUTHERN HEMISPHERES", HE SAID.

MF 1149 23/11 BH

YPAC CORRECTION IN ITEM HEADED '1 FIJI' TIMED 1149

PLEASE READ IN SECOND PARA..... FORWARDS WILL HAVE TO START ALL OVER AGAIN TO LEARN HOW TO RUCK. IT IS ABSURD..... ETC.

THIS CORRECTS MUTILATION.

END JXN 1205 23/11 BH

Libel money to buy new trees

STRETFORD MP Mr Winston Churchill is to devote libel damages won in an action against the magazine Private Eye to a gift of 100 trees to help beautify Trafford Park.

The trees may be planted in an avenue which could be named after him.

The 31-year-old Conservative MP is president of the Trafford Park Industrial Council — Trafic for short — which aims to further the growth of Trafford Park as a major industrial and commercial centre.

Manchester Evening News

PARENTS SACRIFICED SON IN VOODOO RITUAL

Fry a little tenderness

Evening News

Could YOU batter your baby?

It seems incredible, but on Page Seven today you can read about the secret hell some little children are suffering in Britain NOW

£12,000 TO BE WON

News of the World

FIRE KILLS NINE CALVES IN TORO

An 80-year-old man of Kyaka county, Toro, died of stab wounds only a few hours after an elephant had trumpled his son to death. Foul play is not suspected.

Uganda Argus

Defence Minister Moshe Dayan was reported to be keeping a close eye on the explosive situation.

Evening Standard

Hunt for car after Bexhill accident

Police were searching for a car which failed to stop after a mini car swerved off the road and crashed into a lamp post in Magdalen Road, Bexhill.

No casualties were reported, but communications on the 155-mile railway—only link between Addis Ababa and Djibouti have been disrupted.

Evening Standard

PROBATION

At Frome yesterday, Mrs Jennifer Ann Ayres of 5, Duke Street, Frome was placed on probation for three years for steal-the Gas Board.

Bath Evening Chronicle

Another member of the gang, 44-year-old Mr. John Drake, of Oldfield Grove, Rotherhithe, said: "When I saw the stowaway I told the other lads to keep him hidden while I went to our security office.

"We had discovered him when he grabbed the leg of one of my mates. He didn't seem to understand any English. When we asked him with signals how long he had been in the hold he indicated four days by holding up four fingers. The only English words he spoke were National Assistance."

Evening Standard

He said: "If the unrestricted importation and sale of erotic rodents to the public continues, it is not impossible that sooner or later some exotic zoonoses (animal diseases which can affect man) may be introduced into this country.

Daily Telegraph

John Malcolm Green, of Monk's Farm, Burton End, Stansted, was fined £10 by Saffron Walden magistrates last Friday for having no television on November 10. He wrote pleading guilty and apologised.

Herts Essex Observer

TRACES OF WATER ON THE MOON

Front Page

The astronauts, who had been sleeping soundly, were awakened about an hour earlier than planned and told of the problem.

It was quickly traced to an open urine dump valve. This was corrected and the crisis was over.

Back Page

Sunday Telegraph

'Just unbelievable'

While the Air Force band and pipers from Robins A F B in Georgia played such tunes as "Scotland the Brave," "Minstrel Boy" and "The Skye Boat Song" the astronauts made their way to a small stand to make brief speeches.

"It's really great, it's fantastic to be back from the moon," Col. Stafford said. "It was just unbelievable. And it was one heck of a team effort, I mean by 100,000 people."

The London bus is on a world tour, having left Southend on Jan. 23, 1967.

Daily Telegraph

HOUSTON.
"OH, MY golly, you're getting big," exclamed Apollo 10 astronaut Eugene Cernan today, minutes after he woke up and looked down at the earth.

And Cernan looking out of the spacecraft window said of the earth: "You're beautiful. I never thought I'd say that about you, but you sure look good."

The three astronauts, approaching the earth at more than 7,000 miles an hour, after their rings around the moon were woken at 11 a.m. today by a bugle sounding reveille on their radio circuit.

Det. Supt. Bert Wickstead, who worked non-stop for more than 36 hours after he was given a clue to the dead man's identity, already has one man well-known in London's West End helping him with inquiries.

On the isle of Pago Pago, in the South Pacific, a bevy of hula hula girls h a v e promised to dance on the beach when the astronauts land.

Evening News

Surveyor 5 made skid landing

CAPE KENNEDY, Sept. 12.—The Surveyor 5 spacecraft apparently skidded to a stop when it landed on the moon on Sunday.

Times

The judge: "I am glad you told me that. Such criticism that I have made was not criticism of the legal advisers."

The husband was not in a position to attract sympathy in his own methods of investigation, which included searching his wife's drawers and intercepting her correspondence, said the judge

Evening Standard

23

CASANO

**He loved women and women loved
his performance doesn't satisfy**

OVA

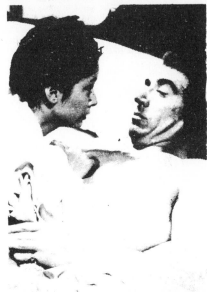

Casanova (Frank Finlay), with Christina (ZMerton), in the first of BBC-2's Casanova "Steed in the Stable."

but –
Whitehouse

25

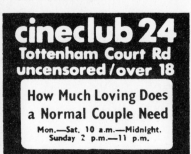

The Hustler Strong, memorable, long and
part extremely brilliant film about a profe
sional snooker player-gambler and his tw
great duels against the greatest hustler
them all, Minnesota Fats. Also, somewha
less successfully related, but still interestin
the story of his sad and sordid affair wit
a polio-crippled, drink-sodden girl of eas
virtue impressively acted by Paul Newma
Rev. Classic; Piccadilly (July 22—28).

What's on in London

Evening Standard

FILM SOCIETY TONIGHT.
Doors open 10.45

HANNES ANDERSEN,
ROLF WANKA
**HE'S AT IT
AGAIN**

Coventry Eveni
Telegraph

Times

Classic Film Guide

The Professionals

Prostitutes and their Clients

Iain Scarlet

The Professionals are Alice, Caroline, Jan, Danielle and Kathy; five women to whom prostitution is a business and a way of life. Simon and Joe are the 'punters', the men for whom the girls exist. All of them have talked to Iain Scarlet, ex-prisoner and founder-editor of *Linkup*. For five years he has known these girls: he has befriended them, walked the streets with them, and has listened to them. They placed their confidence in him; and he has told their stories as they told them to him.

Alice is outwardly a contented housewife, a mother of four, and she loves her husband. At first, prostitution was a way of making up her housekeeping allowance; then it became

from the Catalogue of Sidgwicks & Jackson Publishers
Lord Longford, Prop.)

Unhairy:
Lord Longford, saw "Hair" at the Shaftesbury Theatre in London last night. He said later: "I don't want to discuss the merits of nudity and the like on the stage. I enjoyed the production. The young people in the cast were charming; and there were some moving things."

Grauniad

LEEDS: A new German play including scenes of full frontal nudity and love-making opens at Leeds Playhouse tonight. A spokesman for the theatre said: "It was not until the dress rehearsal that we realised there were nude scenes in the play."

Cambridge Evening News

Ticklish law

The Argus Africa News Service

MASERU, Thursday. — A compendium of Basutoland fishing laws published by a local tourist bureau carries the rider: 'Trout may only be caught on rod and line but Africans are exempt.'

The Torrey Canyon today just before the air assault was mounted on her. Overhead a naval helicopter from Culdrose makes an observation flight.

Shropshire Star

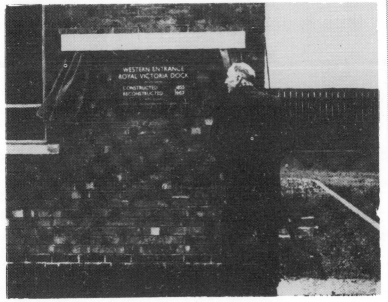

The Chairman unveils the plaque . . .

Staff Journal of the Port of London Authority

Moment of truth: Clapham typist Pauline Leville, karate's highest-graded Englishwoman, makes a scientific attack on Hirokazu Kanazawa, the only man ever to have won the All-Japan championships twice.

DRIVE CAREFULLY in the new year. Remember nine people out of every ten are caused by accidents.

Falkirk Herald

SUNDAY MORNING WITH
Mandrake
Birth control and the single girl

Growing demand for abortion

From the Conservative MP for Chelmsford

SIR In Mr Paul Ferris's article on abortion (13 July) there are two misconceptions

Observer

Three solutions to population explosion—doctor

Cambridge News

THE TIMES EDUCATIONAL SUPPLEMENT 19.12.69

Five girls under 16 have abortions every day

by Tim Devlin

"One thing is certain," says Dr. Gilbert, "sitting on the fence cannot produce any results, and I am personally of the opinion that everything must be tried—including contraceptive advice to the unmarried."

Daily Telegraph

Oldham Evening News

Families with, in all, more than 500,000 children to be better off as from next August through the family income supplement, some by as much as £3 a week;

31

Holiday blessing

Pope Paul, who is spending his summer holiday at Castel Gandolfo, south of Rome, yesterday blessed all those who cannot afford a holiday.

Sun

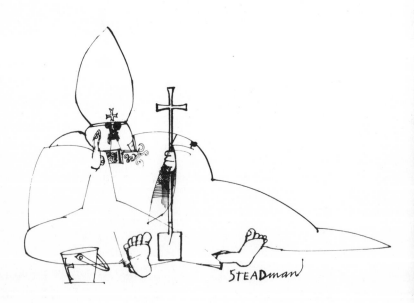

STEADman

'Here Comes the Bride' profane, says Vatican

By ERIC RORICH in Rome

THE Vatican's Department for Divine Worship yesterday advised that Mendelssohn's wedding march and "Here Comes the Bride" should no longer be played at Roman Catholic church weddings.

Mr. Griffin said last night: "I am very pleased after this long wait that we are now able to get married. It was been a long time but it was worth every minute.

Long wait

"The dispensation had to come from the Pope. Now what we both hoped for is actually coming true. Both my wife-to-be and myself were, and still are, true and active alcholics and we will continue to be so.

Yorkshire Post

Pill on altar —pastor sacked

FRANKFURT, Wednesday.— Protestant Pastor Wilhelm Reinmuth has been dismissed for adorning his harvest thanksgiving altar with contraceptive pills. Pastor Reinmuth, in his late 20s, was temporary parish minister.
—*Reuter.*

Evening Standard

Pope escapes

Grauniad

MADRID, (R) — Catholic nuns of the Mission of Jesus, Mary and Joseph, with a television success behind them and Mother Superior Francisca at the guitar, are bidding here for fame and fortune in the pope charts.

New Rites To End Drowsiness During Mass

NIAGARA FALLS — The 776 foot high American side of the Niagara falls roared back to life Tuesday after years of silence.

Evening Post

Heavyweights move in

HEAVYWEIGHT news on the Oxford Poetry chair front: W. H. Auden and Cecil Day-Lewis, the Poet Laureate, are expected to nominate Roy Fuller, the much respected poet (and solicitor), whose recent slimy volume New Poems was received with something approaching rapture.

Times

The death of Sir Walter Worboys in March marked what can be called the end of Stage One of BBC's reorganisation.

BPC Newsletter

ENGLISH POEM ON A SACRED SUBJECT 1974

The subject for 1974 is:

'Thou shalt see my back parts; but my face shall not be seen.'
—Exodus 33. 23.

The poem must not be less than sixty nor exceed three hundred lines in length. The lines must be numbered by fives in the margin. Any metre may be used; but a dramatic form of composition is not admissible.

Oxford University Gazette

I. University Acts

HEBDOMADAL COUNCIL   29 January

Abnormal Psychology is considered an academically important and attractive subject and conditions in Oxford are particularly propitious for the establishment of such a course.

Oxford University Gazette

35

Fugitive is arrested in swoop on cliff villa

Western Daily Press Reporter.

DETECTIVES swooped on a luxury villa on top of 300-ft. high cliffs near Dover before daybreak yesterday, and ended the six-month freedom of Harold Wilson

Wilson woos youth

By our Labour Staff

Grauniad

Man who hit wife
is remanded

An unemployed man returned home and hit his wife on the head, face and body, Bristol magistrates heard.

Harold Wilson, of no fixed address, said he thought she had been "mucking about with some bloke."

He was remanded for reports.

Bristol Evening Post

The 'La Zattera' bed from Cjfra of Italy. Lacquered wooden containers form the bed
structure; the outer covering is in leather and there are compartments for
telephone, clock, books, bottles, bedding and pouf. About £760·00, from Heal's

37

Speaking at Bristol Poly-
technic last night Mr. Wedg-
wood Benn said that these
four barriers were preventing Britain fully exploiting
the skill and potential of its
people.

He said there is a great
revolution under way in education. "My education policy
is to raise the school-leaving
age to 65."

Evening Post

Nice to feel
at home

"I SPENT several days in
a mental hospital and felt
completely at home" **Christopher Mayhew MP**, told a
meeting of the Sheffield
Branch of the Mental Health
Association.

Morning Telegraph

GEORGE BROWN

DEPRESSION
LED TO
SUICIDE
— Inquest told

The Citizen – Gloucest

MR. WILSON.—Members on all sides
have deprecated that those found Guilty
can then obtain large sums of money
by selling their members to the press.

Proprietors generally have expressed
their abhorence of this practice, and I
think it would be better left in the hands
of the Press Council, who are perfectly
capable of dealing with it.

Times

There had been a slight hold-up when it was dis covered that Williams had arrived without his pants

He was, however, accompanied by his father-in-law, a bishop in the Evangelical Church.

Evening Standard

Labour party organisation 'near collapse'

MINE STRIKE BALLET TO GO AHEAD

Britain's miners to go "full steam ahead" with next week's national plt strike ballet.

In Place of Strife Whit

The Secretary of State for Emplo
a discretionary power to require a 28-d
strikes where adequate joint discussions
discretionary power, where a major offici
ballet among its members.

Sunday Telegraph

per on industrial relations

ad Productivity, Mrs. Barbara Castle, will have
ciliation pause " in unconstitutional strikes and
ot taken place.   The Secretary will also have a
is threatened, to require a union to hold a strike

The Times

```
R   PAC EV OVERNIGHT REPEAT

ITV PROGRAMME CHANGE
SOUTHERN TELEVISION
SUNDAY JULY 5,  4.40: THE BIG FILM DELETE "THE PRIME

MINISTER" INSERT "THE RAT"
```

```
London Weekend TV:
Sunday March 26:
6.15pm delete ''The Good Life'' insert ''A Ministerial Broadcast
by the Leader of the Opposition the Rt. Hon. H. Wilson, MP
v-- 25/3 rfh nnn 5 Changes
```

A large piece of green blotting paper rested on the Prime Minister's seat in the House of Commons today. It was both symbolic and necessary.

Times

44

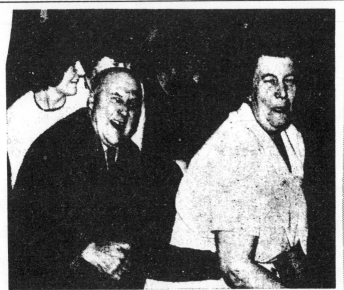

● The only man at Epping British Legion Women's Section annual party at the Methodist Hall on Monday was Mr. A. Freeman. He said he came to do the washing up.

West Essex Gazette

CITIZENSHIP OF Lundy for £25 and small pieces of the island for £5 are to be offered in a bid to save it from commercial exploitation.

Sunday Express

● **PISSOLES AND CHIPS**
After you have prepared your chips why not at the same time fry a couple of pissoles while the fat is still hot?
Together with some salad, cut-up tomatoes and an egg, you now have a delicious hot lunch.

THE TIMES MONDAY AUGUST 13 1956

MORE WOMEN NEEDED FOR RANDOM SAMPLING

FROM A CORRESPONDENT

THE Chancellor of the Exchequer has stated that there is to be an ... children but the woman whose children are away at boarding school can manage ... Food have been widely varied, no ... nutrition reserve later ...

Police inspector Norman Jesty told a reporter yesterday (Friday) "Someone passing the churchyard shortly before 10 p.m. on Thursday, saw the ghost and called us. We went down there and arrested it.

Surrey Advertiser & County Times

Evening Post

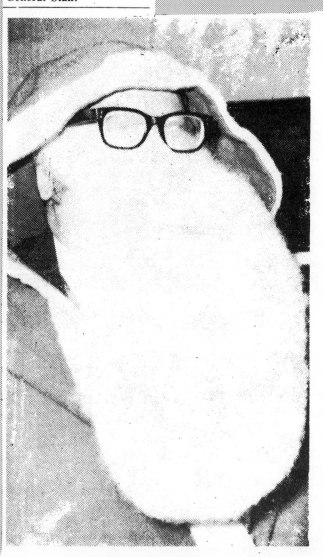

Sir John Verney produced colour photographs to show what the erection would be like. The pictures showed cylindrical structures about five feet high and two feet in diameter, bearing advertisements on their circumference.

Farnham Herald

Hurried away'

he followed two girls of 17 in Binney Street and tapped one on the shoulder. The girls turned, gave a scream and hurried away.

The officer said that he and a colleague ran to the accused, and found that he was exposed. Asked what he thought he was doing, he said, "Nothing, nothing, I was just waiting for my wife."

Hendon Times

The judge said that when the organist started to spend a lot of time at the rectory Mr. Jamal warned his wife "not to get into a position from which it might be difficult to withdraw."

Evening Standard

Q — I am growing up faster than other girls. Do you think I'm normal?
JENNIFER (age 11).

A — YES! Jennifer. I think you are very normal. Some girls develop at an earlier age than others. Do have a chat with your mother about all this. She might buy the booklet "My dead daughter" (price 2/9 —for older girls) which will

Sunday Express

Harris : I understand that you observed your chimpanzees using tools in the wild. Do you think this is another example of reasoning power ?

Goodall : That's a difficult question to answer. It may well have been so on the very first occasion when a chimp used a tool. But today it seems that the youngsters learn to use tools by watching their elders, particularly their mothers, and imitating their behaviour. Of course, it used to be assumed that only man actually made tools as well. But I've often watched them break off a thin length of vine, strip the leaves off, and then, having in this way modified a natural object for a specified purpose, stick it into one of the holes in a termite's nest, wait until the termites begin clinging to the tool, pull it out, and then eat the insects.

Observer

RIDDLE OF THE RUNNER

Clevedon police appealed this week-end: "Tell us quickly if you see the nude runner."

The runner has appeared several times during recent months.

But the police have no means of identifying him.

Dial 999

"He is always naked from the waist down, but he pulls his shirt tails over his head.

"How can you get a description of a chap dressed like that?" said a police spokesman.

He has never bothered anyone. He simply runs past them, turns round and runs back.

"Anyone who sees this man should dial 999 immediately and then we will be able to catch him," said the police

Western Daily Pre

BRUNO BARBEY

What old age has done to de Gaulle

from **NORA BELOFF**: Paris, 29 July

Observer

NEW chairman of the Leicester Swimming Club is Mr. Ivor Finn.

Leicester Mercury

RETIRED doctor Aubrey Westlake is fed up with people asking if his caravan site and holiday centre is a nudist colony.

For 79 - year - old Dr Westlake and his 71-year-old wife, Marjorie, cannot understand what makes people think their Sandy Balls holiday centre is for nudists.

Sun

Television dealers face a £30 million sales loss in the autumn if the Government does not introduce colour for I T V and B B C 1 before Christmas. This was stated by Mr. Brian Proffitt, the dealers' president, at their conference in Brighton yesterday.

Daily Telegraph

Mr Lee Bum Suk, the chief South Korean delegate, cautiously

Times

Simon Dee the disk jockey turned television personality on BBC, will join London Weekend TV when his present contract with the BBC expires Dec. 28. LWT's head of variety programming, **Tito Bums,** said that Dee would host a show beginning in January.

Billboard

Rowland Drewery, a leading fish imported at Grimsby, said yesterday. " The housewife will have to pay, as usual "

Times

CLEAN-UP of the local canal could turn Skipton, Yorkshire, into the Venice of the North, said Mr Arnold Waterfall, president of the town's Chamber of Trade.

Daily Mail

Mrs Robinson, who traces the life of Judas in her book, is the daughter of a Church of England minister. For this work she is using the name Lozania Prole, one of her half-dozen or so pen names.

Daily Telegraph

Haggis hunter

A Scotsman seen crawling along the pavement on his hands and knees in a Camberwell street, told police: "I'm looking for a haggis." He was fined £3 at Balham today for being drunk and told by the chairman, Mr. Walter Dennis: "You won't find a haggis by crawling on your hands and knees."

Evening Standard

51

Evening News Reporter

Kept alive
by a
'miracle'

THERE was no way of saying it gently. The

The report of the Royal College of Physicians, in what is the most authoritative study of smoking yet made, discloses that a man who smokes in middle-age is twice as likely to die before **Birmingham Post Reporters**

NURSE RAPED
By Our Crime Staff

Daily Telegraph
52

New plan for
the Underground
PINCHER: Page 10

CITY PRICES

All taped for next term?
ORDERS BEFORE JULY
1-2 WEEKS DELIVERY

WEST END FINAL
CLOSING PRICES

ACTS BY
Edward Mann
Always making Fashion news

Ebening Standard

TUESDAY, JANUARY 11, 1966

A last gesture of good will—Ayub of Pakistan carries little Shastri's coffin to the plane

All
set
for the
Ashes

JOHN CLARKE'S REPORT—
PAGE TWENTY-SEVEN

KING SAUD TAKES 30 WIVES TO NICE

From Our Own Correspondent

NICE, Tuesday.

King Saud of Saudi Arabia arrived at Nice to-night from Geneva accompanied by an entourage of 84 for a convalescent holiday. People who saw the King leaving his special aircraft said that he looked "very tired."

From

VINCENT MULCHRONE

New Delhi, Thursday

PANDIT N E H R U was most lovingly burned to ashes by his grandson here this evening.

AL-IKHWA HOTEL

TAIZ - Y. A. R.

	LIST FOOD	Riyal	Buqsha
1	Coloured Soop		
2	Fish with Potatoes & Latic		
3	Fish with Eggs & Potatoes Beas		
4	Fish with Beas		
5	Rost Meat with Potatoes Beans		
6	Stick Meat with Potatoes & Beas		
7	Kutlet Meat		
8	Smail Meat		
9	Dry Meat Shab		
10	Stick with Eggs & Potatoes		
11	Kari Meat & Rice		
12	Kari Hans with Rice		
13	Hans with Potatoes & Beas		
14	Hans with Eggs, Potatoes Beas		
15	Liver with Eggs, & Potatoes Beas		
16	Liver with Potatoes & Beas		
17	Hurts with Potatoes Beas		
81	Hurts with Eggs & Patatoes Beas		
19	Mukroni with Eggs Meat Bakred		
20	Bakred Mukroni		
21	Bread with Butter and Jam		
22	Bread with Butter		
23	Sandwish Colured		
24	Sweat Boding		
25	Fruits Coloured		
26	Lce and Tea		
27	Lce with Coffee with Milk		
28	Turkey Coffee		
29	Vimto		
30	Mango		
31	Franch Lemon		
32	Lec-Cream		
33	Drinks Coloured		
34	Orange		

HIS LEG'S IN THE WAY

I AM deeply in love with a Masai boy aged 22. He is strong, virile and handsome, and he has a great brain.

It was only the other night that I realised he has a wooden leg which is screwed on near his thigh. As he is 6' 2" tall this makes him rigid in bed.

I have asked him to remove his leg in bed but he tells me that this upsets his balance. Please, what can I do? I love him so much but his leg is coming between us.

— **Sincerely frustrated.**

Sunday Nation

Half penny's exit

London, June 26 (Reuter)— Britain had ceased minting the half-pinny, the lowest value coin in the currency, Chancellor of the Exchequer Roy Jenkins told Parliament.

Queen Elizabeth yesterday made a proclamation calling in all help-pinnies by July 31 after which they would not be legal tender, Mr Jenkins said.

It is estimated there are about 980 million helf-pennies in circulation.

Today virtually nothing can be bought for a help-penny, twice the value of the now abolished farthing.

Times of India

54

Mr. Goodman expressed his appreciation, and said he did like to feel he could claim some little part in the development of the district. When he came the population was 22,500, and now it was 37,500

Bromsgrove Messenger

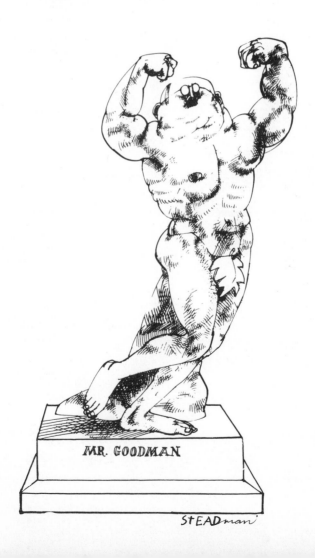

MR. GOODMAN

STEADman

In attempting to def

Bhutto ex

Sunday Standard – India

Jomo stoned at Mboya funeral

Evening Standard

Save

A new swimming pool is rapidly taking shape as the contractors have thrown in the bulk of their workmen to get it ready for use in the shortest possible time.

East African Standard

2½ Indians Are Starving

NEW DELHI, India, May 31

Royal Gazette (Bermuda

his stand

oses **himself**

appointed high court judge

Lagos Daily Times

A period of time was needed before African majority rule could take over in Rhodesia. "And the time required cannot be measured by cock or calendar, but only by achievement."

Middlesborough Evening Gazette

"Home Rule For South"

The independent candidate for the Auckland mayoralty. Mr P. J. Wedderspoon, issued a policy statement yesterday in which he said he believed in home rule for the South Island.

He said his favourite pastime was standing on a haystack abusing sheep.

Woman Dies Of Diarrhea After Attack By Owl

A Nakorn   Srithamma aj
Hosp'tal   patient   died   of

New Zealand Herald

Bangkok World

(Major gold producer of the free world . . . industrial giant of Africa . . . large-scale exporter . . . major importer of European manufactured goods . . . vital link in Western defences . . . scene of a dynamic development in race relations).

Time Magazine

Wine Press – Sussex University

58

PRESIDENT Gamal Abdul Nasser of the U.AR. He is the first Egyptian leader to have wholly Egyptian blood since Jesus Christ. He was elected President by 99.999 per cent of

Ghanaian Times

NIZAM OF HYDERABAD
IS DEAD

Times – Feb 23rd

NIZAM OF HYDERABAD
SLIGHTLY BETTER

Times – Feb 24th

Where will London be by 1980?

A FASCINATING forecast about the future that awaits every Londoner appears in **TOMORROW'S EVENING STANDARD**

Saudi visit by Shackleton

GUNTER PROMISES NEW LOOK AT IMMIGRATION

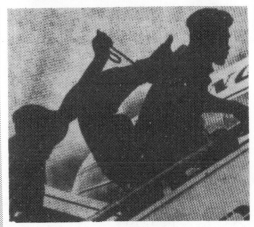

Daily Sketch

Porters march over Asian immigrants

Liverpool Echo

AFTER his girl friend had ended their four years' courtship and broken off their engagement, a 20 years old Ellesmere man embarked on a series of thefts of women's underclothing from shops and clothes lines in Oswestry and Ellesmere, Oswestry magistrates were told on Friday.

Electrician's mate, Geoffrey Morris, of 6, Willow Crescent, was told by the chairman, Mr S. G. D. Campbell: "My advice to you is to pull your socks up".

Marine Commandos patrol N. Borneo jungle river

ROYAL MARINES of 40 Commando patrolling a jungle river in an assault craft in Sabah (North Borneo) near the border with Indonesian Borneo during operations against guerrillas infiltrating from the south. British troops spend periods of up to nine months in the jungle before returning to Singapore. The garrison there was recently reinforced with 500 men from the Rhine Army.

Officer rescues soldier from cliff

A 21-year-old army officer was lowered on a rope 40 down a cliff face yesterday to rescue one of his men, trapped in a gully 100 feet above the sea.

The soldier, Lance-Corporal Edward Hughes, aged 27, of Thornton, Lancashire, was one of 40 men of the King's own Border Regiment, stationed at Heathfield Camp, Honiton, Devon.

Major David Cotton of the Grenadier Guards was bidding on the Prince's behalf. His instructions apparently were to buy guardsmen.

Two lots were purchased: for £12 he obtained the mounted Band of The Life Guards in state dress, including drum-horse and director;

for £9 he obtained six Somerset Light Infantrymen and an officer standing with binoculars, four marching Scots Guards with officer and piper, and seven Grenadiers in firing positions.

Times

Shell found on beach

Indecency probe at Army camp

A warrant officer was arrested last night following an inquiry by Army Special Investigation Branch detectives into alleged homosexuality at the Royal Army Medical Corps Training Centre near Aldershot.

A spokesman said : " He has been put on a holding charge."

Daily Express

Evening Argus

THE FUN'S GONE OUT OF IT, SAYS OLDEST CAMPER (83)

Coulsden & Purley Advertiser

Floodlighting: The Old Admiralty Building looks ravishing at night, with sugar-plum light. All it needs now is a fairy. Whitehall SW1.

Observer

MAN WHO RECEIVED TROUSERS LOSES APPEAL

Eastern Evening News

A feeling has grown up that even some small homosexual incident, since it constitutes a grave moral and social trespass, commits a person to making a definite and defiant stand.

Simon Raven – The Spectator

GERALD MICKLEM CUP		
WINCHESTER	RUGBY	
T. S. Rowan-Robinson (H)	v. A. Swanson (6/5)	- 0
(1 up) - - - 1		
O. J. C. Oakes (H) - - 0	v. K. Irwine - - - 1	
A. J. Bligh (D) - - 0	v. A. Hay (2/1) - - 1	
J. B. Farquhar (A) - - 0	v. A. Poove (6/5) - - 1	
A. M. D. Palmer (H) · - 0	v. R. Jones (2/1) - - 1	

The Wykehamist

Director saw a man in pyjamas —lost control

Camberley News

Mr. Norman Archer at the scene of his complaint.

Evening Chronicle

A BREAK in rehearsals . . . then it's back to the Round Table for Gentleman at Arms Tony Hughes, who is appearing in "Camelot" at the Theatre Royal, Newcastle, this week.

Bridegroom, bride and her new father-in-law

1st Edition

Bridegroom, bride and her new father-in-law

2nd Edition

67

Man found dead in graveyard

Evening Standard

Second Crematorium 'Top Priority'

A SECOND crematorium was urgently needed for Leicester, Alderman Fred Jackson warned.

He said the present unit would not be able to cope with the weight of work much longer. "If anything went wrong we would be in grave difficulties." he said.

Leicester Mercury

Lecturer found

Lecturer Richard Snowdon, 43. missing from his home in Bath, Somerset, has been found dead in a local cemetery

Daily Express

Filming in cemetery angers residents

Evening Standard

CHURCHES should be allowed to remain a sanctuary for bats, and churchyards a refuge for the living wildlife as well as a resting place for the dean, says Mr George barker, a zoologist, in a booklet* on wildlife conservation in church property.

Grauniad

Municipal undertakers have also gone on strike, but a burial "deprived of all pomp" was assured by a skeleton staff.

Grauniad

Bert Barnett was a teacher, and never concealed his opposition to the statutory privileges enjoyed by Christianity in the nation's schools. He formed what was probably the first humanist group in a comprehensive school. Although Mr Barnett had expressed a wish to be cremated, we understand that he was buried with a clergyman

Freethinker

At a meeting to discuss the route of a proposed ring road, the highways committee chairman said: "We intend to take the road through the cemetery —provided we can get permission from the various bodies concerned."

West London Observer

On Wednesday the 23rd (no Communion Service), the Vicar is conducting a Quiet Day for 40 pupils (recently confirmed) from Brentwood School. The Mothers' Union are catering for their physical needs, which are great.

Roydon Parish Magazine

NOTICES

Notice of Churching, Baptism and Marriage must be given to the Rector as long as possible before the day desired, in order to avoid inconvenience to all concerned.

The Rector would be glad if people would let him know when anyone is ill or in trouble, so that he can call at once

INFANT WELFARE

The next clinic will be held on Wednesday, 25th January.

Tne advice of a doctor and health visitor is free to mothers and babies.

God liver oil and orange juice and baby foods at reduced rates are distributed.

St. Peter's Welford-on-Avon Parish Magazine

You and members of your staff

along with your wives

are cordially invited to

The Grand Opening

of

Thake Concrete Burial Vaults

Westport, Ontario

Wednesday, the 22nd day of June

nineteen hundred and sixty-six

R.S.V.P.

Animal Service

Sunday, June 20, at 6 p.m.

in

S. Paul's Church

Covent Garden

(entrance Bedford Street, Strand, opposite Moss Bros)

THE WORLD FAMOUS DOG GOLDIE
who will speak to the congregation on Biblical matters in his own way. Goldie, who has been trained by Marcus La Touche, can also add, substract and divide and is an outstanding example of an animal trained without fear.

INVITATION
Please bring your Pets for the Blessing of the Church: Dogs - Cats - Rabbits - Goldfish - Hamsters - Tortoise - Guinea Pigs or any other animals.

We particularly invite The Guide Dogs for the Blind - The Newfoundland Dog, collecting for Sick Animals - the Police Dogs - and Lady Munnings singing Dog, Toby.

The Service, conducted by REV. H. LEWIS JEFFERSON, will include

Animal Prayers and Hymns,

with address by

Canon CLARENCE MAY: "The Lesser Brethren."

THE WAY WE LIVE
THE COLUMN YOU WRITE

❝At last—I'm first in my husband's life❞
By Mrs. Eileen Dodd

Woman's Own

Evening Telegraph, Tuesday, October 1, 1968—**7**

I HAVE an Irish terrier bitch, which ignores the doorbell. How can I train her to be a watch?

Each time the doorbell rings, jump up excitedly and bark yourself.

THE VET REPLIES

Angry Bull Wrecks Car Of A.I.D. Centre Chief
M. Joseph Petit, head of an artificial insemination farm centre in Aix-les-Bains, France has had his car wrecked by an angry bull!

Leicester Mercury

*Of course, I capitulated—to the dog
with the pale coat and beseeching gaze.*

Cats in church

Faggot & Dyke

Most convents have their cats. When one well-known community came through the cloisters for Vespers their cat often led them to the chapel, his black and white fur matching the Sisters' habits.

Visitors to Walsingham will remember the twin cats Faggot and Dyke. Dyke was somewhat irregular in his attendance at church, but Faggot spent much time there, often sitting on his master's lap during a service and being carried round in a procession.

Church Times

A police dog was taken to the prison and more resin was found inside.

He was sentenced to 12 months' imprisonment to run concurrently with his present sentence.

Times

Fortunately for me at the time when sex was beginning to loom in my life as an enormous and insoluble problem, I began to take an interest in keeping animals.

Armand Denise — News of the World

MAN FINED FOR BARKING

Peter Davies, painter of King Charles Road, Surbiton, fined £3 and bound over in the sum of £10 at Kingston for barking at police dog and being drunk and disorderly.

Evening News

75

Mr. Universe

So who ever broke a leg at golf?

Alan SMITH
EVERY SUNDAY

People

We have often in the past had Wimbledon wobbles with nervy players so shaky · that their boobs have sometimes made park club players blush.

Scottish Daily Express

Bill does it again on Miss Tweedie

RACING

Denis Foley

Evening News

New-heart man plays tennis

Mr Petrus Smith, who underwent a heart transplant operation by Professor Barnard in Cape Town four months ago, has played tennis for 0 minutes.

Evening Times

'Keeper Gary Sprake
leaps for joy at Leeds's
first goal.

SPRAKE demonstrates his
anger after failing to pre-
vent Chelsea's first equalis-
ing goal.

Yorkshire Post

News of the World

Sofia, Bulgaria, Tuesday

**IT REMAINS to be seen whether
Chelsea can make as much impact here
with their football as they have done
with their fashion.**

They have already brightened the grey
countenance of this Balkan city with a tapestry
of colourful ties and skirts.

Yorkshire Evening Post

The latest casualty victim outside right Billy Bingham has a pulle d thing muscle which will rule him out this week.

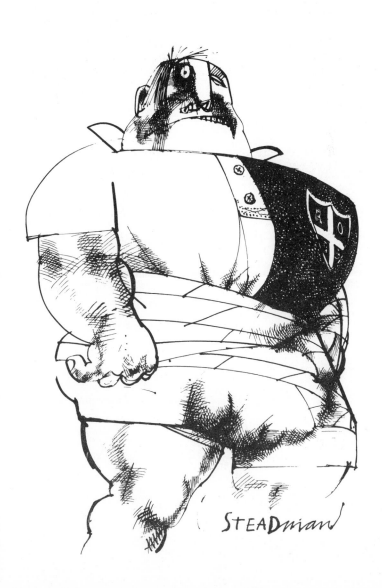

STEADman

Impressive display by Germans

By Cyril Chapman
Aston Villa 0, Southampton 1

Grauniad

⬤ *England players are on a £22,000 bonus if they win the World Cup. West Germany, who are fourth favourites, are on £2,a day spending money, plus ten stamped picture postcards of the Derbyshire Peak district.*

The People

Dead-eye Stewart Fraser, who got three against the league of Ireland recently, attempted a shot from 20 yards, but was so wide of the target that he actually found Carlyle with his attempt. The outside-right was so surprised at the "pass" that he made a mess of his shot at goal.

Banas, who three minutes before had come on for Willim (he went off with an injured bootlace) stole the ball from the West Ham player, took it up the wing and crossed to Sadek who scored by the post.

Monit Sports strengthened their position in Division 2 beating ten-men Ivri 3-0 in a scrappy battle highlighted by the performance of Ivri goalkeeper Stephen Cohen. Athletico Neasden are now three points behind. They dropped a valuable point to Bar Kochba in a 1-1 draw. Roundabout had a 2-0 win over Leytonstone.

Jewish Chronicle

Our women lick male sportsmen

COWES WEEK
DARLING WELL HANDLED
Long reach best

INJURY FORCES MISS TRUMAN TO SCRATCH

imes

Mary's two boobs sink Britain

MARY RAND, the golden girl of the Tokyo Olympics, yesterday dropped the biggest clanger in British athletics—a relay baton that knocked Britain out of the new European Cup competition. Britain's girls were le᙮᙮᙮ semi-final in Fontainebleau ᙮᙮᙮ ᙮᙮ metres relay.

Sun

This does not detract from the achievements of the charging Northants' bowler, whose balls came off the pitches so fast batsmen were hustled into errors.

How England must wish that Statham were just a little younger! Even at 3, however, his consistent accuracy is without equal, and he sets a magnificent example to the younger men under his command.

Grauniad

Venkataraghavan struck a couple of hefty blows before being yorked by Shepherd. Bedi should have been run out, but Dowe, at mid-on misfielded badly and Bedi regained his crease after being strangled half way down the wicket

After a respectable boyhood (born in Keston, near Bromley, Kent, educated at Beckenham and Penge G.S.), Underwood's assaults on county batsmen began in the summer of 1963, when he was nearly 18.

Sun

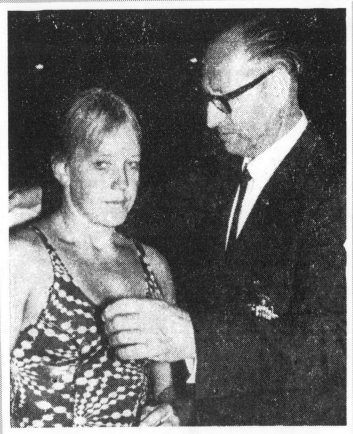

AUSTRALIAN breaststroker Beverley Whitfield is congratulated by team manager Bill Slade after winning the first Test event of the night, the women's 200 metres breaststroke, at Ellis Park last Wednesday. But the Australian joy was short-lived. The Swimboks bounced back to win eight of the 10 events to win the Test easily.

Cape Times

83

POPE'S OPERATION BY NOVEMBER 10th

Talks with Patriarch

THE POPE will undergo the operation in the Vatican for his prostate condition almost certainly by November 10th, it was revealed yesterday. Vatican sources said that the Pope's official artillery, was said to be within 15 miles of Suez city, where thin columns of grey smoke still rose from oil refineries and storage tanks blasted by Israeli gunfire three days ago.

Pontiff soon awake after dawn surgery

OPERATION ON POPE 'SUCCESS'

This picture of the Pope was taken last week in the Vatican.

Yorkshire Evening Post

72 HOURS TO REMOVE ARMS

Nevertheless the Ministry of Works expects that civil servants up to the rank of assistant secretary—there are only three higher grades—will work in the open. And at Building Design Partnership only George Grenfell Baines, the founder of the firm, has retained a womb of his own.

We find there are quite a lot of popils who come from junior schools who cannot spell properly—some of them can't even read

rebel capital said that about a thousand rebels had been seen around the airport, massed in dense brush, and Congolese Air Force planes had straged them with rickets

The influence of television in politics was yet to be seen. "There is at this moment no politician in either party who has any real command of the medium. All one can say is that some politicians are worse than others on television : some are so bad it hurts to see them making such very public schools of themselves."

· The Tories have been under some pressure to toughen up their party political broadcasts. Mr Heath, Mr Macleod, and Mr Peter Walker accordingly reached for their choppers.

Owing to a typographical error, Thursday's article referred to the Soviet military formula which recognised the "futility" of nuclear war. This should have read "utility."

Among the 20 guests was Mr Sellers's old friend and fellow Goon, Spike Milligan. The couple have known each other two years but have always denied they would marry. Mr Sellers has been married twice before.

From Ware. de Rosa went as vice-principal to Corpus Christi College, Notting Hill, where some old hats regard him as a subversive influence. He is reckoned to be an excellent and very professional communicator, not least after defeating celibacy with Brigid Brophy in an early David Frost show.

The other priests who

BOMB IN THE LAVATORY
Police arrest
M. Pesquet

At the time M. Pesquet was himself a deputy, a member of the Poujadist group. The Assembly was not sitting and no one was hurt.

When next you have friends to dinner, one cut up in a mixed salad would be plenty for eight and a novel surprise for one's guests.

Caradon fails to spike Tory guns

Grauniad – July 15th page 1

Caradon spikes Tory guns

continued from page one

Grauniad – July 15 page 26

THE WORSHIPFUL COMPANY OF GROCERS

ON the 9th of May, 1345, twenty-two members of the Ancient Guild of Pepperers, which is first heard of in 1180, founded a Fraternity which became in due course the Grocers' Company. The original members were importers of produce from the East, hence, no doubt, the adoption of the Camel as the Company's Crest.

The Fraternity was entrusted with the duty of "Garbling", or preventing adulteration of spices and drugs, also with the charge of the King's Beam, which weighed all merchandise sold by the Aver-de-poys weight or "peso grosso" and it is probable that the name Grossarius, or Grocer, originated from this fact.

From a dinner menu

MR HEALTH

Sunderland Echo

Walker

PETER WALKER, 38, *was spokesman on Local Government. Housing and Land. Grocer's son.*

Evening News

EDUCATION

MARGARET THATCHER. Age: 44.
lary (as only Cabinet woman): £8,500.
BACKGROUND: Grocer's daughter.

Daily Sketch   89

90

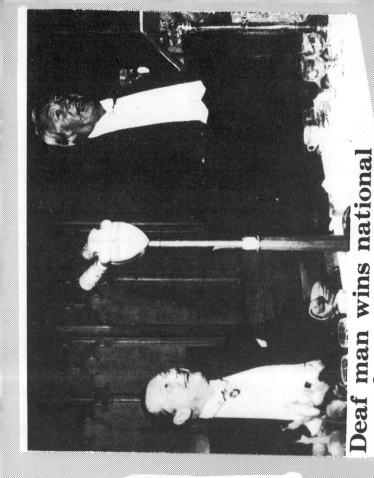

Deaf man wins national speech contest

Topic

SOUTH AFRICAN-born Miss Virginia Rossouw, who now lives at Ashurst Wood, has added yet another beauty title to her collection — the fourth this year. Last week she was chosen "The Prettiest Girl in a Bathing Costume" at the Broadstairs water gala. Miss Rossouw went to collect her prize alongside Opposition Leader Mr Edward Heath, who finished second.

Westham Courier

Ten are arrested near Leeds Town Hall

Evening Post

Mr. Quintin Hogg

Mr. William Whitelaw

Mr. Reginald Maudling

Mr. Anthony Barber

Mr. Iain Macleod

Lord Balniel

Sir Keith Joseph

Sir John Eden

Mr. Geoffrey Rippon

Mrs. Thatcher

GROCER IS TOP OF POPS WITH THIEVES

Joked Mr. Heath: "I never point weapons, but I can think of one chap J could use this on."

He was in a gay mood.

Daily Express

HEATH HOLDS UP HOVERCRAFT

Prime Minister Mr. Heath held up hovercraft full of poeple for 12 minutes today.

Evening Standard

No nighties at Tory dance

A TOWN'S Young Conservatives have cancelled plans to wear pyjamas and nighties at a dance next month. Instead they will go as "tramps."

The dance will be held at Holdenhurst village hall, Bournemouth.

Mr. Arthur Cowley, Conservative agent, said: "The change has nothing to do with the Profumo-Keeler affair. It was decided to change the costume to something more in keeping with the Young Conservatives' activities."

Pop fan Heath at Saucy Sailor show

Daily Express

HAILE SELASSIE MEETS POMPIDOU

Bonjour Selassie

Hullo, Sailor

Daily Nation – Kenya
(Bubbles by Private Eye)

AND SO TO THE BEDSIDE

Reginald Maudling reviews Bedside Guardian 21, published today by Collins, £1.80

I DO not think that I am a very suitable person to review a bedside book, because my trouble has always been waking up rather than going to sleep.

Grauniad

PRAYERS FOR REGGIE

PRAYERS for Mr. Reginald Maudling, who resigned as Home Secretary this week for his part in the Poulson affair, were offered by the Rev. John Ashplant at Stoke Damerel High School for Girls' speech day this week.

Plymouth Times

Life with Powell

By Chris Moncrieff, of the Press Association

The woman behind the most talked about and controversial politician in British politics, spoke yesterday about being Mrs. Enoch Powell.

In an exclusive interview, Mrs. Pamela Powell told me about the man who is still nervous before he makes a speech in the Commons, who finds time, even during a general election, to graft dahlias and mow the lawn, and who reads aloud to his wife in bed every night.

When I asked Mrs. Powell, who is 44, what it was like to be married to such a man, she said: " I suppose you get used to anything."

Times

Intruder in No 10

Manchester Evening News

ANGRY HEATH LASHES TEDDY

Daily Record

NO WATER –
SO FIREMEN
IMPROVISED

Liverpool Daily Post

MONEY CRISIS —TED CALLS FOR CHANGE

Evening Standard

Mr Rippon stated in London this afternoon that he now envisages a time of intense diplomatic activity — "you cannot treat humans like cattle." he told reporters.

After that, the Prescotts called him a sex maniac and said he was "like an animal".

Express & Star – Wolverhampton

Mr Walker began by sending up in a cloud of dust the Prime Minister's promise of 500,000 new swellings by 1970. What were we getting in fact? A mere 365,000 this year and 360,000 next year. And even with the new mortgage plan,

Enter at this point Lord Harlech himself, a drip with briefcases. He refuses tea with which he swears he is awash, says he will read the paper and proceeds to stare fixedly at it, with all the desperation of a drowning man.

Liverpool Daily Post

Grauniad

Premier's tour more stop than whistle

By IAN AITKEN

It was more whistle than stop yesterday when the Prime Minister went round the West Riding on the first of a series of whistle stop tours of marginal constituencies all over Britain.

Grauniad

The Times Diary

Heath's Whitehall scrubbers' party

Times — 23.11.'72 First Edition

The Times Diary

Celebrating a whiter Whitehall

Times — 23.11.'72 Second Edition

Green Shield Catalogue

Evening Press – Dublin

Stirling Moss med seierstrofeet etter et av
sine store løp.

1. ARTIKKEL

«Hold øye med ham, for han blir en av de store!» ble det
sagt om den engelske unggutten Stirling Moss da han begynte
på sin fantastiske karriere som racer-bilist. Etter en seiers-
rekke som ingen kan oppvise maken til, var han utsatt for
en alvorlig ulykke i sitt siste løp, men konkurrentene hyller
ham som en av de største racerkjørere gjennom tidene....

Stirling Moss
-fartsdemon

Sir Charles Clore Millionaire

He has just finished Mario Puzo's novel The Godfather (Heinemann £1·75) which describes methods used by the Mafia. He was most interested.

Evening Standard

LA FEMME-BANDIT DE MARSEILLE ÉTAIT UN HOMME `PAGE 3`

France Soir

'Charm' at 60

Two railway workers, station inspector and a porter, one 63, the other 61, are being sent to a "charm school" to learn how to deal with passengers. It is part of British Railways' brighter and better ·vice campaign.

Reading Evening Post

Trains back to normal

BODY FOUND ON RAILWAY TRACK

Police at Paddington Green are. trying to identify the badly mutilated body of a man, which was found on the track at Paddington Station on Thursday.

He is believed to have been killed by a train.

The man, aged about 55, was 5ft. 8in. tall, with blonde hair and a ginger beer.

Rail commuters in the blackout to Haywards Heath who knew their station by the sound of regular porter William Welfare found themselves getting out at the wrong station when he was suddenly transferred to Three Bridges Meanwhile, Hitler ordered 120,000 German troops trapped south of Kiev in Russia to fight to the death

Evening News

Super train talks

Grauniad

104

TRAIN HITS ARMCHAIR

A train from Ormskirk to Liverpool struck an armchair at Kirkdale. Lancs., last night. Later a train from Liverpool hit a pram at almost the same spot. No damage was done to the trains.

Daily Telegraph

British Rail said it was hoped that from 8 a.m. today a normal service would run, with trains liable to delays of up to 20 minutes.

Times

Special Trains for Ely and Cambridge

Cambridge holidaymakers will be among those to benefit from the special British Railways arrangements to cope with the Easter holiday traffic.

Teenage lovers die

MUEHLDORF, Germany, Sunday.

Two teenagers, whose parents, according to the police, opposed their relationship, lay down on a railway and were killed by a good train.—*AP.*

WIDOW IN BED WITH A CASE OF SALMON, CITY COURT TOLD

Antique dealer thought girl was older

'Stripped' girl—Yard to probe

Standard Reporter

GAS RIG MEN GRILLED BY VILLAGERS

PC saw man squatting on top of wife with raised chopper

China Mail (Hong Kong)

PUNCH COSTS MAN £50

Hull Daily Post

SUICIDE TO GO COMMERCIAL, SAYS BBC HEAD

Daily Telegraph

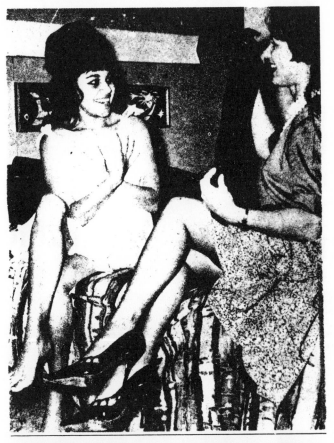

IS YOUR CAREER AS GOOD AS THIS?

RANK:	Sergeant in the Metropolitan Police
AGE:	25
MARRIED:	Yes, with two children
LIVES:	In a modern maisonette provided free
SALARY:	As Sergeant. £1,170 a year rising to £1,255 plus allowances
PENSION:	After 30 years' service a pension of two-thirds his final salary

Crash courses for private pilots

Daily Telegraph

Refuse men get inside support

Grauniad

Bag of 64 in rabies wild life shoot

Yorkshire Post

HE'S A 'ROGER AND OUT' CLERGYMAN

Wolverhampton Express & Star

INTERESTING TALL BOYS AT JAMES ADAM'S SALE

Irish Times

Homosexual Bill

TRYING TO ANSWER YOUR QUESTIONS

The Window

LORD UPHAM FANCIED

By DESMOND HILL

Daily Telegraph

Small organs trendy

Times

TOO DANGEROUS

QUEENS BANNED FROM NARROW HIGH-ST

Bromley & Kentish Times

Where have
all the
pansies gone?

It looked like horticultural sabotage in Luton this week when muscle-men of the Corporation's Highways Department moved in on the Parks Department's pansy patch.

The pansies, neat and spruce on the Biscot Mill roundabout after a day-and-a-half's hoeing, wilted under the onslaught of spades and shovels wielded by the Highways Department workmen.

Luton News

Bernard—
LEVIN

A sight
never to be
forgotten

Bernard Levin
is on holiday

'After
suffering for
months...the
relief is
unbelievable'

wrote
Mrs. B. Sherriff
of Blackpool

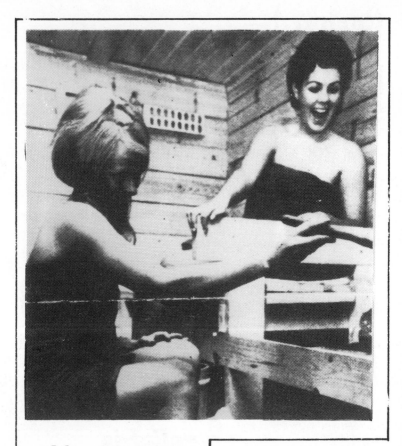

Your own
LOG SAUNA
for as little as
£220
plus erection

A sort of Tory dustbin —Thorpe

Liberals turn against Grimond

By H. B. BOYNE
Political Correspondent

WOMEN'S INSTITUTE

The Harmondsworth Women's Institute held another meeting on 5th April, when there was an amusing talk given by Mrs. Torsten Berg. Her theme was ' Beds I have slept in.' From her talk we gathered that she had travelled all over Europe, and she looked quite charming in her lovely hand-embroidered white cotton nightdress and little cap.

The competition this month was ' How I met my husband,'

St. Mary's Parish Magazine – Harmondsworth

One has to be careful to resist being pompous,and still value highly the honour.   I have decided to put on my notepaper:

    The Sub Dean of Wells
    (The Revd.Prebendary H.L.Franklin)

and people can choose one of three ways of writing to me:

    The Revd.the Sub Dean of Wells.
    The Revd.Sub Dean.H.L.Franklin.
    The Revd.Prebendary H.L.Franklin.

and officially I am addressed as Mr.Sub Dean or Prebendary, but I sincerely hope I shall remain "Preb" or just Harry to all of you.

Parish Magazine – Felton Common

Ash Wednesday is on February 24th. The arrangements are as usual, except that the evening Communion at St. Mary's is put back to 7.30 p.m., to help those whose work prevents their coming at an earlier hour. Now that we have got coffee-making apparatus in the church, I hope that we shall have coffee after the service, so that we can get to knok one another even better.

Parish Magazine, St. Mary at the Wall Colchester

Staff at the electric traction depot at Crewe stopped work yesterday after British Railways refused to negotiate on wage and bonus rates. Mr John Gill, the shop representative, said that the bonus and salary scales paid to the men did not compare favourably with what was paid to comparable grades in outside engineering.

Established members of the corps de ballet are paid on a three-year scale of £12-£14-£16 a week and are believed to be asking for a weekly pay increase of about £3.

(19) PERSONAL

Bromsgrove Messenger

Sunday Times

Gainsborough News

Welwyn Times & Hatfield Herald

Belfast Telegraph

Daily Telegraph

London Weekly Advertise

Sunday Times

Evening Post

Surrey & Hants News

Burnley Evening Star

TELEVISION FEATURES GROUP
AT WORK

Ariel – The Staff Magazine of the BBC

1.30 *Colour : New series*
Watch with Mother
Mr Benn
Every week Mr Benn
dresses-up and finds
himself in a new
adventure

9.0
YOUTH ANSWERS BACK
A Party Political Broadcast
on behalf of the
LABOUR PARTY
Also on BBC-2

Wilson on women—at 10.50

*Novelist Angus Wilson gives a remarkable
one-man performance in Contrasts.*

11.12
SCOTTISH TRANSMITTERS
**I'VE GOT SOMETHING
IN MY HAND**
The Rev. Wilson Anderson
† reflects on something he has
brought to the studio

11.37
SCOTTISH TRANSMITTERS
**I'VE GOT SOMETHING
IN MY HAND**
The Rev. Wilson Anderson
talks to God about something he
has brought to the studio
† Directed this week by
MICHAEL A. SIMPSON

6.55 Stars on Sunday

NINA
ROGER WHITTAKER
GILLIAN HUMPHRIES
LOS PICAFLORES
THE BEVERLEY SISTERS
THE ARCHBISHOP OF
CANTERBURY

TV Times

The Prime Minister : Interviewed by Robin Day on Panorama. (8 BBC-1).

...followed on BBC-2 by **Heart Attack** (8.50).

Observer

Weather service

From next Tuesday, the B.B.C. will include weather hints for mars in the early morning Home Service programme "Farming Today."

Daily Mirror

The most exciting development is yet to come. cently, BBC colour television cameras have been coverg Minstrel rehearsals, and experts are enthusiastic ver the results. Almost certainly one of the earliest rogrammes to be screened in colour will be *The Black nd White Minstrel Show*—adding yet another 'first' to fantastic record.

Radio Times

Michael Miles (46), quizmaster of ITV's "Take Your Pick," who collapsed during rehearsals at Wembley TV studios, Middlesex, on Wednesday night, was stated yesterday to be resting.

He lives in a corrugated iron shack with his wife, three children, a blind mother, and three brothers. He can't read and can write very little. Yet he's one of the world's top golfers. The story of his background and an illustrated description of his swing are in tonight's "Evening Telegraph."

Dundee Courier & Advertiser

7.25 THE SAINT

Girls! Have you ever wondered what **Roger Moore's** legs look like? Now is your chance, for in this episode he wears the kilt! And that is not the only thing to watch for.

TV Times

The BBC Chorus sang with considerable punch in the tutties even if they left something to be desired when individual sections were exposed

Daily Telegraph

11.0 AVENGERS: Escape in Time. Steed visits the barber—and Emma has a close shave !
12.0 THE EDITORS. Leonard Parkin talks to Arthur Brittenden, editor of the Daily Mail. Closedown.

Little Danger Yet of Homes for All

By ARTHUR BOWERS
Property Market Correspondent

Daily Telegraph

SCOTLAND

TO BE SOLD

Property Survey

SANDERSON TOWNEND & GILBERT

Offer for Sale by Private Treaty :

STAINDROP ROAD, DARLINGTON.—An attractive Semi-detached House with double bay window, well placed facing open land close to the Western outskirts. Cheerful and well decorated accommodation including Portico Entrance and Hall, SHitting Room, Dining Room, Kitchenette and Larder, 3 Bedrooms, Bathroom, separate W.C. Brick Garage, Coal Store. Easily maintained Garden. R.V. £92.

Darlington & Stockton Times

BUNGALOW. 3 bedrooms, lounge, dining room, diner/kitchen, bathroom, coloured suite. Toilet 2 miles Andover.

Andover Advertiser

Bristol Evening Post

Fur & Feather, Rabbits &
Rabbit Keeping

tional Children's Bureau

'arents' crucial role in family life stressed

ily Telegraph

Newly-weds, aged 82, have problem

Streatham News

Albert Hall feels pinch

By our own Reporter

Grauniad

Q.E.2 theft: three fined

Daily Express

Richard Burton to teach English at Oforxd

Scotsman

AS the war faded and peace loomed Vera Lynn was able to advise her husband and business manager Harry Lewis that she was going to have a baby. It was a symbolic and logical climax to five gruelling years as a Forces' Sweetheart.

Evening Standard

The army makes it a double

THE first double wedding ever to take place at Amersham Register Office involved three privates and a lance-corporal.

Sir Dallas Brooks (67) arrived back in London today after nearly 114 years as Governor of Victoria, Australia. It was the longest term anyone has served in that office.

Portsmouth Evening News

Mountain patrol shot-up

Miss Alice Bacon, Labour MP for Leeds South-East, was bruised when she fell in the Commons today. She tripped over some dust sheets.

Evening Standard

It was thought that he might follow in his father's footsteps and become a butcher and slaughterer, but he soon left and joined the 1st Battalion of the Middlesex Regiment.

Wembley News

DURING NUCLEAR ATTACK THERE WILL BE A SCHOOL HOLIDAY
—official
By WILLIAM HARROLD

IN the event of a nuclear attack, children will be given a day off school, says the Scottish Home and Health Department.

Log snip ~~~~~~~~~

The Avon and Dorset River Board's annual report for the year ended March 31, 1964, referring to the Piddle, says: "There is nothing to report of this stream which remains, for its size, the purest in the Board's area."

Angling Times

Obstruction

MICHAEL GREEN, of Crimond, Main Road, Danbury, was fined £3 by Maldon magistrates on Wednesday week for causing an obstruction with his ear in Maldon High Street.

Malden & Burnham Standard

ROME, June 20—(AP)— Christian Democrat Senator Giovanni Leone was named as premier-designate Wednesday night and given the task of forming a new government crisis.

Bangkok World

There were no Jordanian casualties, a spokesman said.

He added "Israeli forces opened field gun fire at Um al-idr ford. The Sexchange lasted sporadically for about one hour.

Bangkok World

R. D. SMITH has one Sewing Machine for sale. Phone 66958 after 7 p.m. and ask for Mrs. Kelly who lives with him cheap

26th October

R. D. SMITH informs us he has received several annoying telephone calls because of an incorrect ad. in yesterday's paper. It should have read: R. D. Smith has one sewing machine for sale. Cheap. Phone 66958 after 7 p.m. and ask for Mrs. Kelly who loves with him.

27th October

R. D. SMITH. We regret an error in R. D. Smith's classified advertisement yesterday. It should have read: R. D. Smith has one Sewing Machine for sale. Cheap. Phone 66958 and ask for Mrs. Kelly who lives with him after 7 p.m.

28th October

Tanganyika Standard

, George In loving memory of a very dead Dad, who died April 20th, 1956. "Gently the leaves of memory fall

nephews and nieces.
Floral tributes were: To a loving Wife and Mum. She will always be in our thoughts. Never again in pain. Until we meet, Norman and Roger. From: Stan, Kitt, Jim, Jean and family; Shirley and family and Aunty Betty; God; Mr. and Mrs. Drawnell; Mill, Jack and Martin; Aunty Edie; Auntie Florrie and Uncle Joe; Dorothy, Ted, Pam and Jimmy; Charles; Aunty Doris and

Flower cap for bride

AN Empire-line gown. of bridal crepe with a front panel, bodice, and sleeves of ribbon lace, and an unusual Dutch cap covered with apple blossom holding a full-length veil, will be worn by Miss Kerry McPherson for her wedding in Brisbane today.

Courier Mail – Brisbane

A theatre spokesman said later the wedding would take place in Los Angeles.

Miss Garland (43), and Herron had long been linked romantically. At one time, when they were in Hong Kong, she announced they had been married aboard a ship there, but later the singer told reporters she was only poking and it wasn't true.

She was divorced last year from Hollywood producers Sid Luft.

Audrey Hepburn to marry

Audrey Hepburn, aged 39, is to marry Rome psychiatrist, Andrea Dotti.

Sunday Times

The bride, who was given away by her father, wore a dress of white figured brocade with a trailing veil held in place by a coronet of pearls. She carried a bouquet of rose buds and goods vehicles, leaving free access to all private vehicles not built for more than seven passengers.

Atherstone News

NUDISTS DIVORCED

Wife was " cold "

MR. CHARLES NARROW, 23, obtained a divorce from his wife, Sissy, 16, yesterday, on the grounds of extreme cruelty barely six months after their controversial wedding at a Florida nudist camp.

He said she was cold and indifferent after the first three weeks of marriage. The daughter of the nudist camp proprietor, she wore only a veil and a necklace at her wedding.

STEADman

A Real Chinese Cracker

THE appetising smell of chips drew us to a Chinese restaurant at Penrith. We hadn't much time, so I asked an immaculate waiter if we could carry out. He looked puzzled. I tried again, speaking slowly. Did they have carry-outs? "Ah," he said, brightening. "We have curry chicken. Curry rice. But we no have curry oot." We laughed all the rest of the way to Blackpool.—Mrs N. Lindsay, 6 Gordon St., Greenock.

Sunday Post

ADMIRAL, 93, TO FIGHT DRUGS

Vice-Adml Sir Gilbert Stephenson, 93, and Mrs Christina Custerson, 94, former Essex county councillor, have formed an anti-drug committee because they are concerned that "pushers" are operating near Saffron Walden, Essex.

Daily Telegraph

Sark MoH to resign

Dr. Yeandle Hignell, the only doctor on Sark, yesterday said he was proposing to resign as the island's Medical Officer of Health because he has not been given permission to use an invalid carriage to attend emergency calls.

Mrs. Mary Duncan, who has a food store at Birkenhead Market, was accused at Chester Caste Magistrates' Court of eight offences of failing to comply with food and hygiene regulations.

Mr. Norman Ramsbottom, prosecuting, said two pubic heat hinspectors visited Mrs. Duncan's fruit farm in Long Lane, Saugha, whe she cooked meat for her sta, on September 15.

They found enamel and mincing bows in an unclean conditions, a bocked sink, faulty waste pipes, a bocked basis in inefficient order and walls and ceiling not in

Liverpool Echo

Hijack pilot's wife appeals to Heath

Morning Star Reporters

Blackburn Times reporter Valerie Seaton will not forget the night she danced with Prime Minister Edward Heath at a Young Conservative Ball — and ended up in the maternity ward of the local hospital.

UK Press Gazette

Besides being the biggest bulk carrier to be launched in this country m.v. Siglion is also the longest ship ever built at Laird's. Her length overall is 820 feet.

The naming ceremony was carried out by Mrs. Lill Bull, wife of Mr. Christian R. Bull, partner in R. S. Platou A/S Norway, and, despite her giant size, she moved smoothly into the waiting waters of the Mersey.

Birkenhead News

Rabies law extended to exotic animals

Mr. Heath speaking last night at Croydon.

Times

Mr. Cant : As the upturn in the import cycle is always the Achilles heel of the visible balance, will my right hon. Friend commission a study into the prior deposit system for imports, as no study exists in this country at the moment?

Sir Alec Douglas-Home

The right hon. Gentleman asked about the five principles. I have never seen any difficulty about those principles. The proposals were within the five principles that Mr. Smith and I made, and any future proposals must be within the five principles. I should not at this stage like to commit myself exactly to the method which should be used in regard to the fifth principle in future ; we are looking at the matter entirely anew and completely blind. [HON. MEMBERS: "Oh!"]

NEASDEN

Q8. **Mr. Pavitt** asked the Prime Minister if he will pay an official visit to Neasden.

The Prime Minister : I have at present no plans to do so.

Mr Quintin Hogg

That is why he ᴀs so good humoured and why the Secretary of State for Scotland is busy writing down his notes like a cat that has been at the cream.

Hansard
18/11/68

Pointing at Mr. William Ross, who was preparing to speak for the Government, Mr. Hogg said he looked "like a cat that has got at the Queen".

Times
19/11/68

Your M.P. writes...

LEGAL OBSCENITY

PHILIP GOODHART M P

Beckenham Journal & Kentish Times

What then does the candidate achieve? Has he any part to play? At an election he is the party. He is the captain of the side. He brings the election at least as far as the doorstep of his electors. He can be by his bearing and performance a good advertisement for his party. Perhaps most useful of all he can by his willingness to expose himself publicly either from the back of a Land-Rover, or by speaking at meetings, enable those who might wish to do so to revenge themselves upon their rulers.

Daily Telegraph

EDWARD SHORT, *55, Secretary of State for Education and Science:*
 I work on the box for three hours in the morning, then take it down to the Post Office. There is a tremendous sense of release. I go to the other side of the lake where there is no road, and I have my wife and my dog and that's it. A Minister who is head of a department works at such high pressure normally that this sort of functioning at a lower speed is like paradise.

Observer

Another neighbour Lady Pepler, said: "I was sitting in a deck-chair writing a letter when suddenly there was a loud bang.

"I then went on writing, but after a while it suddenly occurred to me: 'My God, they have got John Davies at last.' "

Sunday Mirror

THERE'S more to being an MP's wife than just attending coffee mornings and opening fetes, as I discovered when I called on Mrs Betty Harrison, wife of Maldon MP Mr Brian Harrison, at Copford Hall, her very English home in the midst of the Essex countryside.

Mrs Harrison is friendly, likeable and easy to talk to. Her dark hair is attractively set, and she has fine fair skin, which, she admits ruefully, comes out in "a mass of freckles" at the first hint of sin.

Her husband is away in London from Monday to Thursday most weeks,

Essex County Standard

SIX MINISTRY MEN FACE CARPET OVER BLOODHOUND

Dealer had smuggled watches

PENDLEBURY market trader Charles Massey, aged 64, was fined £60 at Bolton to-day for having smuggled watches.

Mr. William Hill, prosecuting, said investigations began when a Bolton postman was questioned at Harwich about a watch he was wearing when he returned from a Continental holiday.

The postman said he had bought it from another postman at Bolton. This second man led Customs and Excise officers to Massey known as "Old Charlie.

Questioned Massey, of Boardman Lane, Rhodes, Middleton, said he got the watches "from a man called Abe who comes around the market."

Post Office engineers have put two telephones near his bed, one a direct link with Buckingham Palace so that he can speak to the Queen at any time.

Manchester Evening News

The services of a woman chief inspector in uniform can be had for £14 5s 1d daily (£1 15s 6d hourly) sliding down to £9 8s 4d daily for a uniformed policewoman or £3s 6d an hour. But a woman C.I.D. inspector will cost £13 7s 2d daily

Buckinghamshire Advertiser

139

RUSH BLAZE

POLICE SAID LATER THAT BODY FOUND TODAY WAS NOT THAT OF

MISS JOAN MACSWEEN FROM ISLAND OF SCALFAY, BUT THAT OF A DOG.

SEARCH RESTARTED.

--- OCT 31ST 1200 KS

PAC CORRECTION :

IN PAGE 1 BEATLES, PLEASE READ IN LAST PARA " WE STILL

LUV YA BEATLES ", THUS DELETING THE WORDS " SOD MANILA"

FND 0845 8/7/66 SG

In his dream; he cleaned up Tombstone, broke 100 hearts and the bank at Monte Carlo, and bought the world's smoothest sherry for around £1.

He woke.
And El Cid still cost around £1.

Observer
Sunday May 26th

In her dream; her yacht matched her eyes, millionaires fought duels over her, and the world's smoothest sherry cost around 22/-.

She awoke.
And El Cid still cost around 22/-.

Daily Mail
Monday May 27th

141

Advertisements

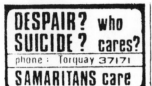
142

Magistrates act to keep theatres open

Evening Citizen

Queen sees Fonteyn take 10 curtains

By a Staff Reporter

Times

STAR'S BROKEN LEG HITS BOX OFFICE

Evening Argus

ROYAL ACADEMY OF RATS
DANTE GABRIEL ROSSETTI
PAINTER AND POET
Last two weeks

Times

Seeking the leak in the Great Train Robbery

Sunday Times

Postmen awarded a £2 million pay rise

Keep Death Penalty, Urges Clergyman

No-one Free From Killer If Deterrent Is Removed

Because of the dreadful crimes of which unregenerate man is capable the death penalty should be there to emphasise the sanctity of human life and protect it

Blind relay team swims Channel

By TERENCE BENDIXSON, our Planning Correspondent

With buildings under construction by two of the most celebrated architects in Britain, Oxford is fast becoming a living museum of modern architecture.

Not tha' ~ent additions ~° al' Many

peaceful water meadows of Mesopotamia.

Coming out of the ground is Alison and Peter Smithson's new building for St Hilda's College. Faced with a motley collection of neo-Georgian neighbours, the Smithson's have taken as their starting point the ima~~~ another aspect of —the golf clu'

THE TIMES EDUCATIONAL SUPPLEMENT

SLOW ACROSS THE CHANNEL?

Peggy Ducros demonstrates the French position

MISUSE OF SEX 'CAUSES SPATE OF TROUBLES'

The Rev. Ray Williams, vicar of Shenstone Parish Church, says he has had a spate of troubles come his way during the past few months through misuse of sex.

Sutton Coldfield News

Lesotho Women Make Beautiful Carpets

By Gordon Lindsay

The Rev. R. G. Williams, curate at Old Harlow, stands at attention while he is wrapped up in toilet paper, during one of the games played at the parish party held by St. Mary's Church, Latton, on Saturday.

SYDNEY JACOBS is expected t his massive tender out in 30 sec

Weekend Telegraph

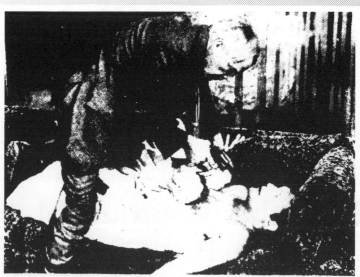

THE JOY OF LOVE: Richard Harris and Vanessa Redgrave are shown in a moment of unbridled happiness in this scene from Camelot. The joy was short-lived, with the arrival of Lancelot, the king and his queen drifted further and further apart. The film is now at the Westmount Theatre.

Five thugs last night pulled the British passenger ship Capetown Castle clear of the sandbank on which she went aground at Flushing early yesterday.

Irish News & Belfast Morning News

Peter Brennan in New York tells how the U.S. sees Nixon's pull-out

President left his options open

Daily Mirror — Sydney

Nixon picks his spot

Evening Standard

McNamara and Fulbright: There are prostitutes in Washington, too

Newsweek

MOTHER-IN-LAW TROUBLE MADE A HUSBAND QUIT

Daily Sketch

You are
Spike Milligan
and I claim
my £5.

en Elizabeth the Queen Mother and Emperor Hailie Selassie of Ethiopia leaving St George's Chapel at
dsor Castle yesterday after the installation of new Knights of the Garter.

(Bubble by Private Eye)

The Queen and President Nixon exchanged gifts of silver-framed photographs during the President's visit to Britain. The Queen's gift was of two coloured autographed photographs of herself and Prince Philip, and the President's gift was a coloured autographed photograph of himself.

The woman, of excellent previous character, was bound over for three years on charges of stealing by finding.

Dublin Evening Press

Picture Robert Hope

THE QUEEN, who was spending the weekend with Lord and Lady Brabourne at their home near Ashford, Kent, returning to Buckingham Palace for a meeting of the Privy Council last night when a State of Emergency was proclaimed.

Shoplifters go on spree in the gloom

The Queen and King Faisal ride through Parliament Square
on their way to Buckingham Palace today.

WOMAN WHO POSED AS 'QUEEN' ARRESTED

Evening Standard

Royal Family bury Duke

The Star — Hong Kong

Have

Your M

, son new members of council.

TO BE HUNG IN MONTREAL

Orm

WEST LANCASHIRE AGRIC

Thursday, 23rd November, 19

IT'S A
WEI
NO ON

good trip,
jesty
DICE OF
he People

THANKS, MAN!

(Bubble by Private Eye)

irk  Advertiser

PER

SKELMERSDALE NEW TOWN ADVERTISER

No. 11,880   4p

OTGUN
NG'
/ANTED

Miss Mary Vincent, Dairy Princess of East Anglia, presents a "Mr. Eastern Counties" trophy to Prince Philip, a competitor from Southend-on-Sea, at a physique contest sponsored by the Milk Marketing Board at Felixstowe, on Saturday night.

East Anglian Daily Times

Prince makes his music selection

ince Charles has chosen his wn music to be performed by he B.B.C. Welsh Orchestra for adio Four's programme "Music o Remember" on July 1, the ay of his incestiture as Prince f Wales, the B.B.C. said esterday.

asgow Herald

Hail, he Prince f Wales

INGS WERE CHANGING AT JCKINGHAM PALACE. SINCE BYHOOD, THE STAFF HAD BEEN STRUCTED TO ADDRESS THE FUTURE NG SIMPLY AS "CHARLES"

UT CHARLES WAS NOW 19 — AND, AID THE QUEEN, HE SHOULD NOW BE ADDRESSED AS YOUR ROYAL HIGHNESS"

heffield Star

TIME & TIDE
THE NEW-STYLE WEEKLY 1'-

PRINCE CHARLES: THE ROYAL EXPERIMENT

The Prince meets his tenants

BY A STAFF REPORTER

The Prince of Wales, aged 18, showed signs of having inherited his father's sense of humour yesterday when he asked a publican: " Do they drink a lot on this island ? "

william hickey

For Charles on his 21st, a birthday gift called Freckles . . .

Daily Express

Royal artist Pietro Annigoni, who recently painted a controversial portrait of the Queen, with his protege Romano Stefanelli

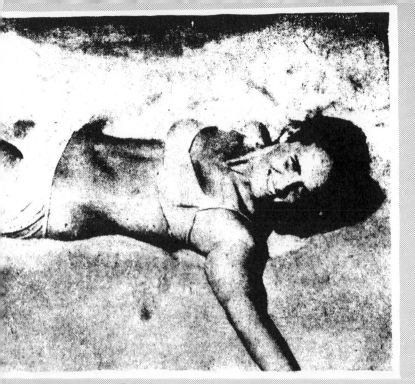

ily Sketch

Shepherd to paint new royal portrait

AT 69 years of age, the Queen Mother is to sit for another portrait. And this time the artist is David Shepherd, who has made his name as a wildlife painter.

'I'm delighted,' he says. 'It's a great chance to get away from painting elephants.'

Daily Mail

One of the boys who shook Prince Philip's hand said: "He's quite a character. I told him we came across a dead deer during a 39 mile route march in Perthshire to gain the award. He cracked back straight away 'Did you eat it?'"

Daily Telegraph

Winner of the leather Queen Mother as a competition prize at last Thursday's Christmas Fair held by the Friends of Richmond Royal hospital was Mrs. Spicer, of 77 Lower Mortlake Road, Richmond.

Teddington & Hampton Times

houses we also inherited. One third have no fixed baths, or piped hot or cold water. And many have sanitation unchanged since Queen Victoria sat on the throne.

Ted Bishop MP — Labour Woman

Queen Victoria paid a visit here, but only briefly and because she could not wait until she reached Erlestoke Park six miles on.

Wiltshire Times

An employee at the North-West Castle quoted Prince Philip's Secretary as saying the hotel for the peasant-hunting holiday starting November 25 was chosen on the toss of a coin.—AP.

S.C.M. Post

It is typical that when on holiday at Sandringham earlier this year he shot so many peasants that the market experienced a glut. During George VI's time

Wee hoose

"Must" for **Prince Andrew** on Balmoral holidays is plenty of play time at nearby Birkhall, the **Queen Mother's** residence.

For in its garden stands the Wee Hoose, a thatched highland cottage in miniature, built as a toy when the **Queen** was a child.

minor magic

One attraction is that "the fairies" usually leave intriguing offerings there: bags of sweets, or cakes all ready for a party.

Like most grannies, the Queen Mother enjoys arranging minor magic when she knows small visitors are on their way.

Woman

Boys set on prince's party

PRINCE Andrew, 11-year-old son of the Queen, was one of a party from Heatherdown School, Ascot, attacked by East End schoolboys who demanded their pocket-money.

The incident happened in the Natural History Museum, South Kensington, in March, but has been kept a close secret until now. The East End boys were playing truant from school.

The Prince was not personally part of the museum.

Evening Standard

An address of welcome in Welsh was made by the president of the Eisteddfod Court Sir Thomas Parry-Williams. Sir Thomas said the court of the National Eisteddfod of Wales, with its council and Gorsedd, begged leave to offer to the Queen their loyal thanks and greetings upon the most gracious visit to the National Eisteddfod being held in the beautiful town of Llandudno.

" We rejoice in the thought that your presence will enhance the dignity of this national institution whose main objects are the fostering of the Welsh language and its literature and the promotion of the rats in Wales, the land whose name we are proud to recall being borne by your Majesty's eldest son, His Royal Highness the Prince of Wales," he said.

THE DUKE PRAISED

Turning to the Duke of Edinburgh, who was wearing a grey suit, Sir Thomas said the Eisteddfod most cordially welcomed the Duke also. He himself had been invested an honorary ovate of the Gorsedd of Bards at the Cardiff Eisteddfod in 1960, taking the title Philip Meirionnydd.

" His Royal Highness's support for all those activities which make for the betterment of the British people is known to all, and is highly Thomas.

Staff are instructed that a passenger giving the following name and address must NOT be permitted to travel without payment:

H.R.H. PRINCE ANDREW VIII,
Banstead House, Belmont.

Conductors and O.M.O. drivers are instructed to add this name and address to the list of passengers not to travel without payment, which is in their possession (issued in Traffic Circular No. 80, Item 1235).

London Transport
Traffic Circular

Automatic sewage works at Looe

Sewage plant on sea front might smell, expert says

Times

"I am married to a sewage worker. My small son, aged four, pulls the chain after going to the toilet and announces with pride that its on its way to daddy."

Evening Mail

FARMER'S EIGHT-HOUR VIGIL IN BOG

All that night Sharkey remained in the bog without refreshments or food of any kind.

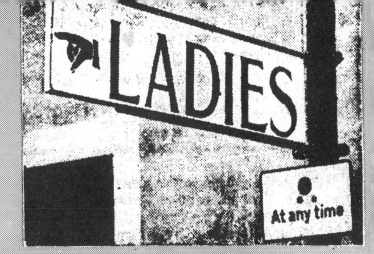

163

Man Threw Sewage Over 74-year-old Neighbour

STORY OF HOSTILE ATMOSPHERE

ERNEST SYDNEY QUINN (65) emptied six buckets of sewage on his garden—the seventh he threw over his neighbour 74-year-old Mrs. Dorothy Eleanor Walding.

" The lack of toilet facilities is absolutely disgraceful," he said. It was time the Labour Government did something about them.

Mr. PEART, Leader of the House, said he was well aware of all this. The only solution was a major reconstruction of the House or a new Chamber.

Daily Telegraph

Symphony

AT THE CORONATION of the Queen the Ministry of Works fitted up a line of extra lavatories in Westminster Abbey for the hundreds of peers assembled there.

Sun

School lessons in the lavatory

By our Correspondent

Overcrowding is so bad in the village school at Cefn Mawr, near Wrexham, that a class takes its lessons in the lavatory. A Denbighshire education authority official said yesterday: " the children will not have to endure conditions like this for long. A new £700 toilet block is to be built."

Grauniad

THE BATTLE of the loo at Watford High Street station continues. The rural parish council has decided it will not take British Rail's decision sitting down.

Evening Echo

THE toilets at the Harry Pollitt Memorial Youth Centre are nearly complete. Book now for socials, schools, work weekends, etc. Details: 16 King St., WC2 or 01-504 9367.

Morning Star

16

MAN FOUND IN MERSEY

Wallasey Police issued the following description of a man whose body was recovered from the Mersey, near New Brighton, yesterday morning: Age between 30 and 40, 5ft. 9in. tall, good build, tattoo on left forearm of woman kneeling on a chair holding a fan, wearing dark striped suit, two print shirts, woollen vest, grey socks and black boots. The

STEADman

NOTICE

A NYONE taking the un-authorised use of my bull on my farms in Kirlish, Killowen and Curraghmulkin will be prosecuted without exception. Signed, William B. Nethery.

Tyrone Constitution

NOTICE

I, A. PAGE, 38 Mogford Street, Mackay, did not on the 25/4/64 wear anything but war medals. Persons spreading reports otherwise will be prosecuted.

Daily Mercury

Yasha Van Dyke & Lola
KNIFE THROWERS

At the Neasden Empire wish all their friends and acquaintances a very Merry Christmas and a Happy New Year.

Evening News

PERSONAL

Nabil, come home, your mother forgives you and your brother is going to be president of the Badminton Club. Your Finaneee, Tu-tu.

Outlook (American University of Beruit)

NOTICE

Will Mrs. Hargreaves, of 13 Coates Avenue, and all persons in it with her, please return Mrs. S. Hogarth to her own home at 2 Apple Tree Cottages, Salterforth, or legal action will be taken.

Signed, S. HOGARTH,
2 Apple Tree Cottages,
Salterforth.

APPEAL

Mr Cameron said: " I am not going to sell dirty books. There will be stimulant creams, contraceptives, vibrators, pills, sexy nighties and artificial sex organs . . . but nothing kinky."

Scottish Daily Record

LOST by Sir John Laing, Fair Holme. Marsh-lane, Mill Hill, N.W.7, Blue Budgerigar. Answers to " Billy." Says " Good morning, Sir John," " Good morning, Lady Laing," etc.—Telephone Mil 3636, 9-5.30. Ext 14. Z

Situations Wanted

YOUNG LADY aged 16½ years, interested in children, seeks part-time employment for ten minutes. High School education. — Write Box 393, Standard, Skegness.

Skegness Standard

SPIRITUALIST NATIONAL CHURCH, Spen Lane. Owing to unforeseen circumstances Mr. O'Dwyer's meeting for Wed., 23rd, has been Cancelled

...ychiatric training student, Mrs. C. R. C. Benton, of Upton, receives the Fred Nutter Memorial prize.

Oldham want Raper

Times

Raper says 'No' to £56 a week at Oldham

Halifax Evening Courier

'Orange a day keeps flu away'

by CHRISTINE DOYLE

Observer

PAISLEY AS OMBUDSMAN

A SUGGESTION that the Rev Ian Paisley be appointed ambudsman for Ulster was made at Down County Council's meeting in Downpatrick yesterday by Major R T. Bunting.

Down Recorder

Mr. Joshua Cardwell (U., Pottinger) said he believed the processions were spontaneous and that no action should be taken against their organisers.

Captain O'Neill said it was not clear if it was an isolated act of terrorism of "the beginning of another campaign of violence."

The mobilisation of 1,000 B Specials — they are part of a 10,000-strong farce — began last autumn when about 200 were

Ulster wills

£8,167 — Mr. Edward Hamilton Kennedy, of The Anchorage, 9 Norwyn Ave., Donaghadee, lighthouse keeper, who died April 25 last (duty in Northern Ireland £344).

£5,047 — Miss Harriette Florence Ward, of 35 Osborne Drive, Belfast, who died on April 4, 1966. She left £100 to Drumbeg Parish Church, for the upkeep of family graves.

The magistrate, Mr. G. C. Lynn, said he thought everyone had been the worse for drink.

Belfast Telegraph

TO BE HEAD OF
R.U.C. P.R. SERVICE

Mr. Read Armstrong, Public Relations Officer of the Northern Ireland Pigs Marketing Board since 1964, has been appointed head of the Publicity and Information Services by the Police Authority of Northern Ireland.

Irish Times

Mr. Ivan Neill (Ballynafeigh) replied favourably to the first question, and on the second said he would use his influence to ensure the preservation of the Lord's Dad.

Belfast Telegraph

The Ould Sod

Eamon de Valera, Ireland's President. In earlier times he too raised money in America.

Financial Times

```
PA

snap correction:

In 35 Soldier (1335) please read

in line 1:

   Miss Bernadette Devlin MP etc.

This substitutes ''Devlin''

for ''Devil''.

end cxn 1356 9/8 pl
```

Belfast chosen as model city

The National Society of Christians has selected Belfast as the " Model City of the World, 1970."

The Society, which is based in the USA, says that Belfast " possesses a zealous Christian attitude and participates with an active interest in religious functions."

Belfast Newsletter

NOTE

In some of our copies the article *The Power of the Papacy* described the Pope as 'His Satanic Majesty' this should read 'the Roman Antichrist'.

Protestant Telegraph

MILK RACE

It's a strong strategic base for next week's operation, but unfortunately Bayton, who would have been Edwards's natural deputy, is still suffering from his fall. He finished at New Brighton with the bunch, but his back still pains, and he felt every bump in the road.

It was Havelka, a Czech of whom we know very little, who opened

Observer

Advertisement

They padlocked the gate to the area and agreed to forgo their own rights of admission to the green.

All except former London architect Christopher Press, 31, who arrived after the deal was concluded.

He says he intends to have his wife, his three children, his friends and his pet cat on the lawn any time the fancy takes him.

People

Questioned about Kissinger's whore abouts, Ziegler said the president's national security affairs adviser was in the White House Monday.

Saigon Post

The judge said: "There was a succession of boy-friends. Each time she would trundle her bed into the kitchen, shut the door and remain there for a substantial time.

Then the man would leave, and she would trundle the bed back in the bedroom and go to sleep. It must have been extremely embarrassing to this husband.

It is possible she just wanted to sit and chat to the boy friends and took the bed in because of the lack of furniture," said the judge.

Sun

Mr. Justice Brabin.—Would any nurse in the normal course of treatment knee a man in the groin ?

Mr. Banks.—Not under any circumstances.

Times

Lady Roborough fancies pigeons

Western Morning News

It seems from Carreras' research that to please women the product must be long, slim, mild, cheap and preferably packed in gold.

Daily Mail

The solution of Janet's pregnancy, with Terry deciding it wouldn't be so awful after all to marry her, was natural and pleasing. So was the way that Rose—excellent performance by Patricia England—lit up and expanded when made love to.

Observer

It is evidently not a favourite question in Government circles. Clapping his telescope to his blind eye, Sir Alec saw no First Lord of the Admiralty — which was doubtless excusable as there is no First Lord any moe. Since Easter he has turned into the Minister of Defence for the Royal Navy. Not that Sir Alec was making any quibble over that ; L o r d Jellicoe is Lord Hellicoe, what every title he may sail under.

Slim chicks lay better

Grauniad

Purchase Tax Exemption on Young Children's Knickers, Panties and Briefs

THE COMMISSIONERS OF Customs and Excise have issued the following rules for the guidance of traders and Officers in applying the exemption to knickers, panties and briefs, having regard to changes in style and design.

The question of further amending the criteria for exempting these garments is under review in consultation with the national trade associations concerned, who have also been consulted prior to the issue of this Notice.

The rules are as follows:

(a) **Measurement.** The method of measurement specified in Notice No. 78A cannot be achieved by measuring the garment from waistband to crutch and multiplying by two. The measurement should be made panel by panel, and should not be restricted by the presence of any ruching.

(b) **Marking.** Regarding the upper limit of the exemption, knickers, panties and briefs marked or catalogued 'W', 'M', 'Medium', 'Maids', 'Junior Miss', 'Teenage' and the like are outside the scope of the exemption.

(c) **Style.** The exemption does not extend to styles not generally suitable for young children's wear and for garments to receive relief under item G.21 of Notice No. 78A they should, except as noted below, be in plain styles – i.e., in single colours and non-decorative. The presence of lace edging of up to $\frac{1}{4}$in. width, even if in contrasting colour, is not regarded as of itself taking the garment out of the 'plain style' category.

However, the following three categories may be treated as within the exemption as far as style goes:

    (i) frilly party knickers (which have the frilling across the back);

    (ii) babies' and infants' knickers, panties and briefs; and

    (iii) knickers, panties and briefs which are either printed overall, or patterned overall, subject to the additional measurement limit of 40in. fully-stretched waist. This measurement should be taken across the waistband stretched to the full extent of the elastic from one side to the other and multiplied by two.

Knickers, panties and briefs with lace etc. inserts or panels, and bikini briefs are chargeable in all sizes.

Board of Trade Journal

(g) The decision of the chairman on any point shall be fatal.

Standing Orders – Institute of Journalists

★‡AMENDMENTS TO THE POST OFFICE GUIDE, JULY, 1966 EDITION
(Last amendments appeared in POC 14.6.67)

PAGE 47
PROHIBITIONS
    Line 1. After Contraceptives; *insert* fresh meat and other food-stuffs:

Mrs Jacqueline Onassis arriving at Hyannis Airport, Mass, yesterday, with her daughter Caroline (right), 11, and son, John, 8, and other members of the Kennedy family for the funeral of Mr Joseph Kennedy. Caroline injured her forehead in a riding accident a fortnight ago.

Kennedy family mourn their patriarch

Dear Sir,

I think the enclosed photograph is the greatest photograph in the history of journalism.

        Sincerely,
        SPIKE MILLIGAN
Orme Court, W 2.

NO THANKS

SO AN American doctor thinks
that men over sixty years of age
should have two wives, does he?
Well, I for one wouldn't want a
dirty old man of sixty to share
with some other woman, thank
you.—*Mrs. N. G., Ewell, Surrey.*

Sunday Mirror

The *Aristide Case*, morally serious, intellectually well-contrived, continuously suspenseful, is never as bathetic as the worst or as moving as the best of *The Brickfield*. I had for it the sort of admiration that I have for Joe Davis playing snooker, an astonished delight at the playing of each shot for the advance of the score and the positioning of the next. Technically it is a splendid achievement. But Miss Jameson is not playing with balls, but with characters whom she has deliberately shorn of the awkward protuberances that make human beings run false to prediction.

Financial Times

Tall, good looking, brown eyed, soft voiced, with a large capacity for listening, she is the daughter of the late Philip Graves, who was on the foreign staff of *The Times*, and a piece of the poet Robert Graves. Her family is far flung, much cousined, and delightfully eccentric.

Times

DAILY LIFE SERIES

2 *Daily Life in Florence under the Medicis*
J. LUCAS-DUBRETON

'A vivid evocation of that warm terracotta city . . . the sources are rich and numberless . . . an absorbing picture.' *New Statesman*

'. . . a full, compact and useful guide to French society during the first 15 years of the nineteenth century.' *The Daily Telegraph*

George Allen & Unwin

Facts show that the nature of the Nobel prize which the Soviet people call a "tool of the West" has not changed, but Sholokhov has already completely discarded the fig-leaf with which he had covered his nakedness and stands completely revealed as a "tool of the West." The reactionary bourgeoisie has finally found a more useful "traitor of the East" than Boris Pasternak.

Peking Review

easden Hospital affair

We regret that owing to a pographical error the closing ntence of Sir David Llewen's article yesterday apared as "Blessed are the erciful, for they shall receive oney." "Money" should have ad "mercy."

eading Evening Post

Apologies to the Seventhay Adventist Church, Chisck. In our "church notes" st week we stated that the urch had observed a day of prayer and feasting. This ould have read "a day of ayer and fasting."

rentford & Chiswick imes

r REGINALD BIRCH

We are asked by Mr Reginald ch to correct a misprint in issue of 8 April '71 as a ult of which Mr Birch was cribed as the "Facist" mem of the engineering union cutive. The correct adjective, written in our Industrial Corpondent's report, should have n "Maoist."

ily Telegraph

Ir. Stephen Boulding, whose e was inadvertently misspelt in week's report of the Young servatives' conference at Eastrne, asks us to state that the ase he used in his speech in a mless mock-serious vein was ogs and Italians". Owing to error in transmission this was rted as "wogs and Italians".

unday Telegraph

The oddly gifted Hungarian painter to whom I last week compared the Belgian artist Spillaert was called Csontváry (1853-1919), and not Conservatory.

Observer

A correction

In a caption in last night's Evening Gazette, Dorothy Duffney, conductor of the Cleveland Musical Society, was described as Mrs. Vera Beadle. She is, of course, Mrs. K. Atkinson, of Hartburn Lane, Stockton.

Evening Gazette

CORRECTION: *In our Morley College feature on March 15, this painting was published inadvertently in the wrong position. We apologize to Robert Medley, the artist. This is the correct presentation.*

Illustrated London News

Nine more held at Portman Rd.

NINE FOOTBALL FANS were arrested in Ipswich on Saturday during the Ipswich-Liverpool championship clash, bringing the total number of arrests at Portman Road this season to 131

They are: Mr. George Cunningham, a signalman with British Rail, of Mill House, Bramford; Mr. Harold Phillips, a clerk with British Rail, of Ipswich Road, Needham Market; Mr. John Turner, a retired newsagent, of Homewood, Station Road, Haughley; and Mr. Peter Erbe, self employed, of Gardeners Road, Debenham.

Ipswich Evening Star

MR. S BUTTERS for reasons of ill health, is permanently discontinuing widow cleaning

Cambridgeshire Times

Labour candidates: an apology

It is regretted that in some copies of the Main Town edition of yesterday's Evening Star details of Labour Party candidates for four seats on the new Suffolk County Council were inadvertently used with the introduction to a report about football fans being arrested, under the heading, "Nine more held at Portman Road."

APOLOGY

An Advertisement in the Evening Chronicle of 19th September, 1972, carried the sentence "Pot in the Park" — This should have read "Pop in the Park." We apologise to the Top Rank Suite, Sunderland, for any inconvenience caused by this error.

Newcastle Evening Chronicle

THE BLACK DWARF

DIARY OF EVENTS

Monday, October 14th

ANGRY ARTS FILM SOCIETY:

Cuba Si — Chris Marker's partisan documentary of the aims, the mood and the rhythm of People's Cuba.

NEWCASTLE SOCIALIST SOCIETY:
1 p.m. Union Debating Chamber. Speaker: *Tariq Ali.*

NEWCASTLE VSC:

7.30 p.m. Old Assembly Rooms. *Tariq Ali on the October Mobilisation.*

Tuesday, October 15th

EDINBURGH: VSC.

7.30 p.m. Hume Tower.

Tariq Ali on Vietnam and its implications for Revolutionary left in Britain.

Wednesday, October 16th

DUNDEE UNIVERSITY LABOUR CLUB

1 p.m. University Building.

Tariq Ali on The Collapse of British Social Democracy.

GLASGOW VIETNAM AD-HOC COMMITTEE:

7.30 p.m., Typographical Halls, Clyde Street.

Tariq Ali on October 27th Demo.

Thursday, October 17th

STRATHCLYDE UNIVERSITY VSC:
12.30 p.m., Union Hall.

Tariq Ali on VSC.

GLASGOW UNIVERSITY R.S.A.:

7.30 p.m., Men's Union.
Tariq Ali on 'Student Power'.

The second session was held in McMillin Hall after the liberal Students for a Restricted University had offered to book the place in their name. After the performance of some "revolutionary" music, a sonata for flute and piano by Pierre Boulez to which little attention was unfortunately paid, the French delegate's predictions came true and serious faction fighting developed

Black Dwarf

TO ALL GRADES OF NURSING STAFF.

IN 10 DAYS TIME ON THE 20th OF OCTOBER THE MINISTER

OF HEALTH WILL OFFICIALLY OPEN T.B.3. ALL RESIDENT

STAFF ARE REQUESTED TO PLEASE LEAVE THEIR ROOM DOORS

OPEN AND TO SEE THAT THEIR ROOMS ARE TIDY.

PLEASE LOCK ALL VALUABLES AWAY IN A SAFE PLACE.

Notice in St. Alphege's Hospital, Greenwich

Because she has a leg in plaster after a skiing accident. Queen Juliana of the Netherlands swore in the new Cabinet at her Palace yesterday.

Liverpool Daily Post

Birthday Honours announce

Mr. **Cecil Geraint Ames**, president of the Sierra Leone Court of Appeal and president of the Gambia Court of Appeal, who lives at Bath, becomes a **Night Bachelor**.

**Bath & Wilts
Evening Chronicle**

CENTRAL CHANCERY OF
THE ORDERS OF KNIGHTHOOD

St. James's Palace, London S.W.1.

The QUEEN has been graciously pleased to award the **Royal Victorian Medal (Silver)** to the undermentioned:

Yeoman Bed Goer Arthur ADAMS, Her Majesty's Bodyguard of the Yeomen of the Guard.

Paul Beard, ten, of Woking, Surrey, was rushed to hospital at Chertsey last night—to have a peanut vending machine removed.

Daily Mail

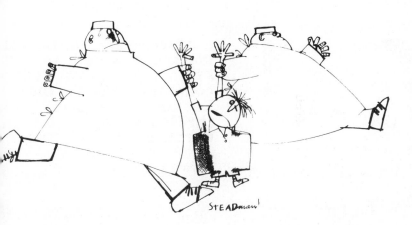

Spotted man wante questioning

Hackney Gazette

Mr. JUSTICE CUSACK . . .
saw for himself.

JUSTICE TAKES A TRIP

Western Mail

America's millionai
platinum king ' flew t
Atlantic to watch Nijins
conclude his business
England in a style whi
thrilled a huge crow on
warm, sunny afternoon.

Sunday Mirror

Man broke speed limit to save pregnant cat

Richmond Herald

M4 contract for Mo

A. Monk is expected to be awarded the contract for a 12.2 mile stretch of the M4 motorway from Liddington to Wickham worth about £7.25m.

CONSTRUCTORS' WORLD

On the bottle

A bottle of whisky and a bottle of sherry, together worth £3 16s. were stolen by a gurglar who forced a window of a house in Granfield Avenue, Radcliffe-on-Trent, last night.

Nottingham Evening Post & Standard

Bodies in the garden are a plant says wife

Hong Kong Standard

EVENING NEWS, Monday, December 2, 1963—5

THREE BATTERED IN FISH SHOP
Man gaoled for assault

Evening News

THE Ford Foundation announced today that it is giving $85 million (£30,356,000) to some 50 leading American symphony orchestras.

At a Press conference in New York today Mr. Henry Heald, the Foundation's president, said one-quarter of the grant would be given on a no-strings basis.

Daily Telegraph

Spare our trees—they break wind

THE whole character of Bognor Regis as a holiday resort could change if a plantation of 60ft.-high trees at the west end of the town is cut down for housing development.

This warning was given yesterday by Mr. Edmond Venables, chairman of Bognor branch of the Wild Life Association.

Said Mr. Venables: "The trees are very densely planted and give a terrific amount of protection from the south-west and westerly gales. A 60ft.-high tree can break the wind for up to one mile.

Evening Argus

Weather checks

THERE WAS LESS weather than usual last month.

Bristol Evening News

?

Our weightlifters need more support

185

SQUATTERS IN COURT AFTER SIEGE

The magistrate, Mr. Edward Vicarage, Leyton, was mounted on Saturday, with all the accuracy and timing of a military exercise.

Leyton Express & Independen

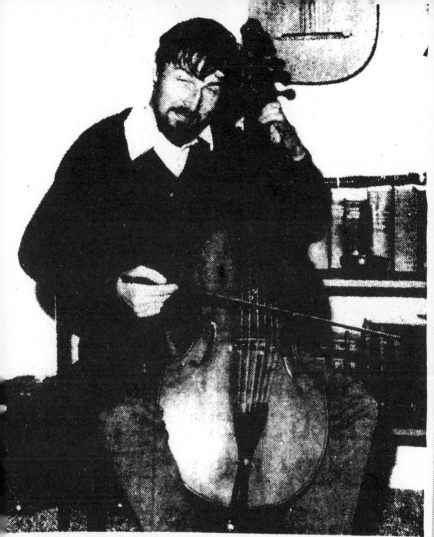

Alf Chapman casts an expert's eye over one of the tomatoes he judged at the Rose and Crown gardeners' show

Better than sex

Sir,—I am not a Welsh teacher, but love my country and my language very dearly.

Learning Welsh at school did me no harm, as I received equal marks in both languages. Welsh and English (full marks).

I think that Welsh is far more pleasant and useful than sex, of which people seem to get so much of these days.

J. Jones,

Caergybi,
Sir Fon.

Liverpool Daily Post

Prison conditions

From the High Sheriff of Essex

Sir. Your leader on April 5 " Four Years after Mountbatten Report " inferred that repression is the order of the day in H.M. Prisons. I visited Chelmsford Prison last week and my impressions were very different. In the maximum security wing, not only were the security measures most efficient and effective but at the same time the atmosphere was relaxed—indeed the prisoners were watching horse-racing on television. Each prisoner has a cell to himself with a bedside light and is allowed to keep a transistor radio.

In the workshops, prisoners were doing useful and interesting jobs, such as learning to be tinsmiths, rather than being subjected to the monotony of sewing mail bags. In the vocational training section, prisoners were being taught the art of copper beating, and I saw some examples of excellent craftsmanship.

Times

'GALLANT KITH AND KIN'

Sir.—I take this opportunity to express my full agreement with Mr. Hamilton's letter on the subject of Rhodesia.

What I say is: Three cheers for British common sense at last! I certainly did not fight in two world wars to see this criminal treatment of our gallant kith and kin.

If Harold Wilson and his hirsute supporters wish to misuse in this fashion folk who have displayed so inspiringly the new much abused spirit of Dunkirk. I say: Let them foot the bill and grapple with their own uneasy consciences. Decent folk want no part of it.

The treatment of Rhodesia. one of the last bastions of decency on the Dark Continent. is typical of the atheistic. immoral malaise which threatens this country.

While we have men like Mr Hamilton. unafraid to speak their mind. Britain may remain what she is.

HERBERT GUSSET
(Lt.-col., Ret.)

The Old Mill House,
Nr. Essendon.

Potter's Bar Express

An invitation

If you feel strongly about any particular subject why not write to the "Gazette" about it.

Or if you have a point of view to express, drop a line to the Editor. We prefer discussion on local, rather than rational, topics.

County Times & Gazette

Gang-bang

Sir: A few weeks ago, my husband and I went to a party in Neasden, being given by my husband's boss, an insurance broker. The door was opened by the boss's wife, who, much to my husband's astonishment and my shock, wasn't wearing a stitch of clothing. I was embarrassed, distressed and angry, but what can you do when your husband's boss and his wife are involved? I pretended not to notice a thing.

Men Only

The hunted stag

" Reading about the unfortunate stag hunted by the Devon and Somerset Staghounds last week brought to my mind the cruelties that go on all over England to defenceless animals and children.

" I wish the law would tighten up and for every case of cruelty by these sadists give imprisonment and a severe lashing with the cat."

EVELINE BRASIER.
15, Chudleigh Road.
Alphington, Exeter.

Express & Echo

Cheerful choppers

□ Why is it, I wonder, that butchers always seem cheerful? It's not that their job is a specially enviable one, for in cold weather meat must be very cold to handle. Maybe they get rid of any bad temper by bashing away with their choppers? **Mrs. J. R. Stevenson, Southampton, Hants.**

Woman's Own

Health succeeds where MacMillan, Wilson failed --Britain will join

By Anatole Shub
Washington Post

Bolton Sunday Gl

THE COMMON MARKET
SWISS ROLE FOR BRITAIN ?

Evening Standard

THE COMMON MARKET

The Controversy rages
Throughout Our Ancient Land
And pages upon pages
Come readily to hand
Of Whether we should join or not
This happy, happy Band.

The Dont's and Anti-Marketeers
Are howling forth their Woe
Expressing all their doubts and
    fears
Of Whether we should Go
Into this Wider Fuller life
Where richer harvests grow.

So brothers, Stand United be this
    our Joyful Song
Come into the Common Market,
    with Heath we can't go wrong
So boldly let us enter before it is
    too late
And Join the Common Market
This truly blessed State.
                    R. G. A. ETCHES.

190

BIRTHDAYS TODAY

Admiral of the Fleet Sir Varyl Begg, 60; Sir Albert Bennett, 68; Air Commandant Dame Helen Cargill, 72; Sir Eric Coates, 71; Rev. Dr. Austin Farrer, 64; Mr. Laurence Harvey, 39; Mr. Stanley Holloway, 78; Mr. Justice Lloyd-Jacob, 71.

SIR ERIC COATES

Sir Eric Coates, C.S.I., C.I.E., who assisted in the liquidation of the abortive groundnuts scheme in Tanganyika, died on Saturday at the age of 70.

Times — October 1st 1968

British penalties for cheating in potato-growing contests are among the severest in the civilised world. — SAPA-Reuter.

Gaberone Star